praise for *earth angels*

"Sandy's book is a gift. It's a reminder that in a world filled with challenges, kindness and integrity are the superpowers we all have. *Earth Angels* has inspired me to lead by example and look for ways to lift others up every day."

—**Kim W.**

"*Earth Angels* is absolutely brilliant. Sandy Lundy is a masterful storyteller, whose deeply personal reflections and inspiring call for kindness illuminate the profound impact ordinary acts of compassion can have in the face of life's greatest challenges."

—**Lisa F.**

"Having experienced a tragic loss myself, *Earth Angels* gave me hope. Sandy turns her personal pain into purpose, reminding us that even in grief, kindness can heal and inspire. It's a book I'll return to time and again."

—**Jessica M.**

"I love *Earth Angels*. This book guides readers through all the feelings—including the discomfort that we all experience and struggle to embrace when someone has passed away. I couldn't put this book down, and you won't want to either."

—LeeKei E.

"This book is a must-read not only for every parent but for every person! It is raw and gut wrenching at times but brutally honest. We are all human a.k.a. 'perfectly imperfect.' Ms. Lundy forces us to look inside ourselves and think about our own actions. Sometimes even the smallest positive action can have a wonderful effect on someone else."

—Debbie C.

"Sandy Lundy's *Earth Angels* shows us that ordinary people can do extraordinary things. This book is full of stories that uplift, motivate, and challenge us to make the world a better place, one act of kindness at a time."

—Rick R.

"This book is going to change many lives."

—Sandra R.

earth angels

earth angels

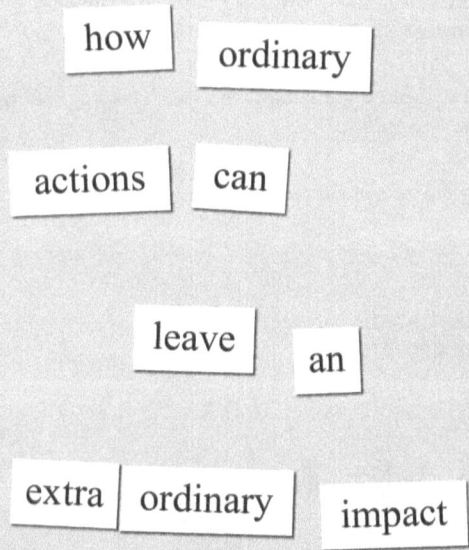

how ordinary actions can leave an extraordinary impact

sandy lundy

Copyright © 2025 by Sandy Lundy.

All rights reserved. No part of this book may be used or reproduced in any manner whatsoever without prior written consent of the author, except as provided by the United States of America copyright law.

Published by Advantage Books, Charleston, South Carolina.
An imprint of Advantage Media.

ADVANTAGE is a registered trademark, and the Advantage colophon is a trademark of Advantage Media Group, Inc.

Printed in the United States of America.

10 9 8 7 6 5 4 3 2 1

ISBN: 979-8-89188-018-4 (Paperback)
ISBN: 979-8-89188-020-7 (eBook)

Library of Congress Control Number: 2025904678

Cover design by Matthew Morse.
Layout design by Ruthie Wood.

This publication is designed to provide accurate and authoritative information in regard to the subject matter covered. It is sold with the understanding that the publisher is not engaged in rendering legal, accounting, or other professional services. If legal advice or other expert assistance is required, the services of a competent professional person should be sought.

> Advantage Books is an imprint of Advantage Media Group. Advantage Media helps busy entrepreneurs, CEOs, and leaders write and publish a book to grow their business and become the authority in their field. Advantage authors comprise an exclusive community of industry professionals, idea-makers, and thought leaders. For more information go to **advantagemedia.com**.

To my Three Little Birds.

contents

introduction 1

chapter one 5
the high five

chapter two 27
childhood bullying

chapter three 37
the other b words

chapter four 51
the call to lead by example

chapter five 73
our selves

chapter six 87
cultivating kindness online

chapter seven 113
finding your superpower

conclusion **135**
*embracing the earth angel within
and inspiring kindness*

remembering shane resnick **141**

acknowledgments **149**

about the author **151**

in loving memory of … **153**

The stories shared in Earth Angels *are based on personal memories and experiences. For privacy and confidentiality, some names, locations, and identifying details have been changed or edited. While this book is intended to inspire and uplift, it is not meant to provide professional advice or guidance. The purpose of these stories is to celebrate the impact of kindness and encourage readers to reflect on how ordinary actions can create extraordinary change.*

introduction

The warrior knows that her heartbreak is her map.
—GLENNON DOYLE

Can you find meaning and purpose for your life after tragedy? Can you look for the angels on earth—the people who make a difference in the lives of others—even when every cell of your being has been crushed? Can you be a positive force, even after you have experienced deep loss?

I think so. And it was my intention in writing this book to encourage kindness in the world—even if when we look around us, it's hard to see the good because the bad and the unkind are so noisy. I'd like to start a social movement—and be a force for positive change.

Like my son.

It's important that I preface this book by making it clear that what you are about to read is by no means intended as a cry for sympathy. The world has never been at a loss for bad things happening to good people, and I am no exception.

I do not want anyone to feel sorry for me. I want this book to be a catalyst for change.

You will read about my crusade against bullying and hurtful behavior—from the playground to the boardroom and beyond. From the casual cruelty of kids singling out another child with verbal (or worse) abuse to adult tantrums, rude behavior, bad bosses, and everything in between. But, at its heart, it's a mission to encourage and celebrate those angels among us who try to lead their lives by example—with kindness and integrity.

You will also read about the tragic reason why I am so passionate about this cause. But let me assure you, I fully understand that not a single person on earth breezes through life without challenges, pain, struggles, failures, and deep loss, yet it's what we do when we meet these challenges that makes the difference. No matter where we come from, we all actually have much more in common than not. When faced with obstacles, we can fall down and get up or fall down and give up. Many of us have heard the adage that when a baby is learning to walk, they will fall many times. The baby doesn't just lie there and give up. The baby gets up and tries again. And again . . . As humans, we are born preprogrammed with the ability to overcome obstacles. We don't fail; we temporarily fall.

> *Our greatest glory is not in never falling, but in rising every time we fall.*
> —Confucius

This book took many years to write, but its contents represent a lifetime. I've tried to escape, but I can't get away.

So, in lieu of feeling sorry for myself, I've reflected upon every obstacle I've faced as each having a reason—a purpose, a lesson. As a result, I have discovered the amount of love that I am capable of giving and receiving. I consider this a gift. Don't get me wrong; there are countless days and nights when I'm a hot mess, lying isolated in a fetal position, crying for mercy. Perhaps it is my body's way of purging the pain. Who knows? But I make a conscious effort every day to become better, not bitter.

It's time for social change. As a human being, every person reading this book has a vital and rewarding role to play in helping to make this change. I believe it can start by simply leading by example—whether that's leadership in the workplace or an act of kindness for a stranger. It's the little things we do each day that make a difference in attitudes, thinking, and behavior.

Every day, we are each faced with choices. Choose to set the example. Choose to empower others. Choose to live by integrity. Choose to help lift others up. With this commitment, we can each have a meaningful impact on the lives of everyone around us, including the people who work with us, our customers, our friends, our families—and, ultimately, everyone around them as well . . . A ripple effect.

We can all start with (and within) ourselves, and it can start with a smile, or, as you will soon understand, a simple high five. I am deeply grateful that you have chosen to read this book.

chapter one

the high five

earth angels come in all ages and sizes

*I've learned that people will forget what you
said, people will forget what you did, but people
will never forget how you made them feel.*
—MAYA ANGELOU

You could hear a pin drop.

That always happens when I tell this story.

Whether at a school, fundraiser, parent group, or corporation, this is the story that makes people stop, listen . . . and think. It is the story that makes the room fall silent. It is the story that causes a gasp.

It's my story. But it's a story that has become much bigger than I am.

Several years ago, a neighbor asked if she could drop something off in my mailbox. Her son Luke, who was in elementary school at the time, was in the car. As she approached my driveway, Luke suddenly shot up in the back seat and excitedly exclaimed, "Mom! Mom! A really nice boy lives here! He's the only kid on the bus who's nice to me. Every single day, he gives me a high five."

Luke was talking about my son Shane.

What Luke didn't know was that, two weeks prior, Shane had died by suicide.

At age eleven.

Apparently, Luke was being relentlessly bullied both at school and on the bus. Thankfully, he reported what was happening to his parents. Unfortunately, the school wasn't doing enough to help Luke, so his parents decided to take him out of that school and give him a fresh start at another.

It's silly, sometimes, the things that trigger bullies—the smallest idiosyncrasy, an element of appearance, or a unique trait that labels a kid as "different" and subjects them to unnecessary ridicule and pain. For Luke, it was simply because he loved superheroes.

I later learned that Shane was also being bullied. There were no warning signs; I had no idea. I am the worst-case scenario. Out of all the things that I've learned since Shane has been gone, I know one thing for certain: If this can happen to me, it can happen to you.

Shane *loved* musical theater, particularly Broadway theater. It was something we did together as our "special dates." I cannot tell you how often he listened to the soundtrack of *The Phantom of the Opera* (and countless other shows—the benefit of living close to New York City and its theater district). Every note, every line of lyrics, memorized, appreciated, and adored. Every musical we attended, I had to remind Shane not to sing out loud. He knew every single word. In fact, when Shane died, the cast from *The Phantom of the Opera* came to sing at his funeral. According to the cast, Shane was "one of them."

Shane was *that* person. He was an Earth Angel. People picked up on it—he was a light.

CHAPTER ONE

A breathtaking moment captured backstage at The Phantom of the Opera *on Broadway: Shane wearing the actual Phantom's mask, his eyes sparkling with joy and wonder. This unforgettable experience was made possible by Annette Lovece, a cherished member of my Club Med family and a true Earth Angel. Annette played a pivotal role in igniting Shane's deep passion for Broadway theater, nurturing his love for the stage and its magic. This photo is more than just a memory—it's a testament to the power of kindness, inspiration, and the lasting impact of those who help dreams come true.*

I will always be left to wonder how or why anyone could be bullied for simply having a passion for something so positive and beautiful. You see, when Shane was giving Luke encouragement, he knew exactly what it felt like to be picked on. Shane was that kid, that person. He wanted to help Luke feel special, even though he was apparently also living in his own silent pain and fear. For the rest of my life, I will be haunted knowing that my son, my baby, was in so much pain that he felt taking his own life was the only way to escape it. Had I known what was happening, I would have never let him go.

You may be wondering what happened to Luke. Thankfully, Luke thrived at his new school. In fact, Luke was given a citizenship award in his first few months for helping another new student navigate his own first days.

It is a universal truth that kindness is contagious.

Yet, Shane was not afforded that opportunity. Shane's death was a metaphorical tsunami that has forever scarred not just my life, but the lives of all the people who loved him—his father, his grandparents, brothers, cousins, aunts, uncles, friends, and the many people whose world he touched with his gentle nature, sincere kindness, and inner light.

What was left after the tsunami was utter devastation. The landscape of our lives has been permanently and irrevocably destroyed. Totally unrecognizable from the world we lived in before his death.

However, I truly believe that when we come to the worst moment of our lives, we have two options. My own decision was quite stark: I could choose to stay in the devastation—or I could try to heal the landscape.

Healing is a never-ending process of the ebb and flow of tides of grief and occasional moments of clarity. One of the worst things about having been inducted into a club I have no desire to be in is that I never know when something will trigger my grief. The triggers are always unexpected and always feel like a hard punch in the gut.

One of the many things that shattered me and kept me up at night was, at first, the pain of wondering how I could not have known Shane's inner hurt. Shane was the kid everyone thought of as full of sunshine and joy. For Shane, there was always a positive way to view something, regardless of the situation. Shane never saw a glass as half

CHAPTER ONE

full or half empty. To Shane, the glass was always full because, as he shared with me once, "The other half is just gas, so technically, the glass is always full." There was always a bright side. Always. And he was always thinking of others.

I remember spending a day at a local Chamber of Commerce community event with live music, games, and activities. I noticed that Shane and his older brother Griffin had won a few of the team races, and it was nice to see them working together, laughing and enjoying themselves. As the activities were ending, I noticed the woman who had been leading all of the kids' activities walking toward me. As she approached, she asked if Shane and Griffin were my boys. I immediately tried to think of what they could have done wrong. As the mother of three boys, that was not uncommon. But it looked like everyone was having a great time, and my boys were so happy. My immediate response was skeptical: "Yes. Is everything OK?"

She replied, "I just wanted you to know what your boys did. They won many of the games, but instead of keeping their prizes, they conferred with each other and decided to give all but one of them away to share so that all of the other kids could also have a prize."

That experience exemplifies Shane and his brothers. Yet, I'm left to wonder why Shane did not give any indication of what he was going through and his personal anguish. When he was sick, I'd always make him chicken noodle soup and nurse him back to health. Yet, this particular pain was different—it was silent. Hidden. It wasn't anything I could gauge by taking his temperature. I'd give anything, including my own life, to be able to take that pain away from him. I'll forever be haunted, wondering why he chose not to speak up.

Perhaps he was too scared, embarrassed, or proud. I'll never know. Even in hindsight, I could not pick up on anything. Perhaps it was because we were so close that he didn't want me to worry. As a single mom, at dinner time, I wouldn't eat until the boys were finished. I always needed to ensure they had enough to eat, and I would have whatever was left. Shane was the kid who knew I wouldn't eat my own dinner until he and his brothers had finished. Every night, he kept some of his dinner on the counter, claiming his belly was full, knowing that what was left would be my dinner. He was very wise beyond his years.

My mind also relentlessly churns with the idea of *What if?* What if a teacher had noticed Shane was being bullied and done something about it? What if someone had paid Shane a compliment when he needed it most? What if he had simply been offered a kind word, a warm smile? A simple high five? What if someone had stood up for him? What if I'd never let him get on the bus that day? But I've come to recognize that I've been looking at it backward. I was viewing life through a dark lens of the past—something I could not undo. I could ask *What if?* forever, yet nothing would change. I can't bring him back, and I couldn't take away his pain. The crushing, guttural feeling I wake up with every day and go to sleep with every night, like a heavily weighted blanket, can't be resolved by asking those questions and trying to figure out what I could have done differently in the past. So, eventually, a different notion began to take shape in my mind. Clarity didn't happen immediately. It was mixed in with all the turmoil and hurt at first. But then I started searching for my higher ground.

You see, when a tsunami rushes in and devastates a place, people desperately seek higher ground in order to survive. They reach for branches or passing debris to keep them afloat. They climb hills and mountains, looking for safety. Looking for light.

I knew I had to keep myself afloat. I instinctively knew I needed to survive. If I'm being honest, it wasn't for me. It was for my boys, Shane's brothers. In the aftermath of my grief tsunami, I struggled to

CHAPTER ONE

breathe, to merely exist. I felt that I was drowning, desperate for air, and my only way to breathe was through a single straw sticking out of the dark abyss. I lost friends. I figured out who "my people" were and who was there for me and my family. But eventually, I clawed myself to higher ground, and that higher ground was a powerful thought that began to take place, like a lone tree on a hillside after the storm subsides.

Survival.

Rather than looking to the past with *What if . . . What if I looked to the future?*

What if I could seek a way to make sure that what happened to Shane never happens to another person—another child? To help all the Shanes of the world, the Lukes of the world, those who just want to fit in and be liked (and people like me, as you'll read in the next chapter).

What if I did everything I possibly could to ensure this never happens to anyone else? As you read this right now, there are millions of people of all ages, all over the world, suffering in silence.

> *It's no use going back to yesterday, because I was a different person then.*
> —Lewis Carroll

The Birth of a Movement

I knew I had to find a way to keep Shane's memory alive and to share his indelible fingerprint of love and kindness. At first, I delved deeply into research, trying to figure out what I had missed and how I hadn't recognized that my son was in such pain. I quickly learned that, more often than not, bullying goes unnoticed and/or unreported. It breaks my heart knowing how many people, and far too many children, have lost their lives because of the words and actions of others. So, I started my mission to help kids, particularly kids who have been or are being bullied. I created a 501(c)(3) called Shane's Imagine-Nation.[1] I will talk more about this later in the book, but there was no doubt in my mind that I wanted to find a way to inspire others to spread kindness. It was a goal to expressly help kids understand that they are perfect, just the way they are. That each of us has unique gifts to bring to this world, and the world is a better place because we are all in it. That one simple act of kindness always leads to another, and then another, and so on. Kindness is contagious. Here's our mission:

> *Shane's Imagine-Nation is a registered 501(c)(3) nonprofit corporation created to help kids (especially those who are/have been bullied) build self-esteem and recognize their great worth. With an emphasis on kindness, starting with self-kindness, our mission is to empower kids to do the right thing (knowing that it is often the hardest thing to do) and to understand that they make the world a better place simply because they are in it.*
>
> *We are all perfectly imperfect.*
> *Kind is the new cool.*

I began with a variety of grassroots initiatives at local schools and community organizations. I tell Shane's story, and the story of the high five. I've created "Kindness Clubs" and always try to recognize kids who have made a difference in their schools, communities, or families—through kindness. For these kids are the true superheroes of the world.

---

[1] "What We Do," Shane's Imagine-Nation, https://www.shanesimaginenation.org.

CHAPTER ONE

> *That's the only way to describe him, like lit from within.*
> *—Jessica, on meeting Shane*

One of the most difficult things, I've found, is dealing with the questions I dread the most, those most commonly asked between adults: "Do you have kids?" or "How many kids do you have?" To this day, I'm still not sure how to answer. I doubt I'll ever know how to answer. I've also found that people tend to act (and react) differently when they speak to or meet a parent who has lost a child. They may avoid the grieving parent altogether because it is painful to even *imagine* losing a child. (I can't tell you how many times people say to me that they cannot imagine the pain. In short, no. They can't. And I'm glad for them because I really don't want to imagine it either.)

Others may think they should not bring up the lost child because it is too painful for the grieving parent. That is categorically false. You see, the worst thing for a grieving parent is to think that their child will be forgotten. Yes, it's incredibly painful to speak about Shane, to have to live and breathe every day on this earth without him—but he *lived*. And he had a positive impact on so many people—all over the world. He was a real person who loved and was loved so much. It would be far more painful for his name to fall silent on my lips. I only wish he had loved himself as much as, or more than, he was loved.

I want him to be remembered. And so, I share his story because I believe he has many lessons to teach us.

Then, I had another profound observation.

What About Adults?

Maybe it's me, but I've always been able to spot hypocrisy and phoniness from a mile away. And, after my son died, my "bullshit" meter became finely tuned.

Bullying, in all its forms, thrives on falsehoods—whether it's the illusion of power, superiority, or control. Combating it requires something far more powerful: sincere kindness. Grief has taught me to see through the layers of pretense that people often wrap themselves in. When you're grieving, you become acutely aware of what is real and what isn't. The empty compliments, the fake smiles, the shallow gestures, the air kisses, or the unsolicited advice about what you *should* do lose their meaning. I've learned that true support isn't about words or advice; it's about action. It's about being there when no one else is, offering help without being asked, and showing up with sincerity, not judgment. Grief strips away the phony masks people wear, revealing who genuinely cares and who is just going through the motions. And, in the same way, kindness cuts through the cruelty of bullying, dismantling its false power with genuine empathy and caring. When we offer kindness—real, authentic kindness—we can begin to heal from both grief and bullying and to help others do the same.

As I looked at the circumstances of Shane's experiences of being bullied, and reflected upon my own experiences, it struck me that this problem is far, far greater than anyone, to my knowledge, has ever really written about or explored.

CHAPTER ONE

Excuses, Excuses: The Problem with Downplaying Bullying

Many adults carry antiquated mindsets about bullying behavior. They often associate bullying with the more visible and aggressive behaviors of childhood, such as name-calling, physical confrontation, or overt exclusion, and believe that these actions diminish with age. These outdated notions fail to account for the more subtle and insidious forms bullying takes in adulthood. As a result, many adults overlook or dismiss behaviors such as manipulation, exclusion, or passive-aggressive actions as harmless or, in a professional environment, simply "part of the job." This narrow view prevents them from recognizing the damage caused by bullying behavior, which often manifests through power imbalances, social isolation, or undermining someone's credibility. By clinging to these archaic definitions, adults inadvertently allow harmful behavior to persist, normalizing toxic environments and silencing those who suffer in the face of more sophisticated forms of aggression.

Our children (and I don't mean *mine,* or *yours,* but the world's) see us, watch us, hear us . . . learn from us. And, oftentimes, what kids see is not healthy, and when we see this bad behavior, we don't call it out. There are plenty of examples of adults acting poorly, often setting a terrible example for the children who are watching and learning from their behavior. Here are a few scenarios that highlight these moments:

Sporting events: I'm willing to bet that if you've ever been to a youth sporting event, at one point you've witnessed parents or coaches losing their temper, yelling at referees, or berating their own children—or kids on the opposing team. Children who witness this may internalize that losing is unacceptable or that it's OK to disrespect authority figures when things don't go their way.

Social media: If you are on social media, I'm also willing to bet you've seen adults engaging in name-calling, spreading misinformation, or blatantly disrespecting someone with opposing views. Children often see these interactions and might believe that it's normal to degrade or insult others online, encouraging the next generation to repeat this behavior in their own digital spaces.

Political discourse: In today's polarized political climate, it's not uncommon for political figures and their supporters to engage in vitriolic debates that involve personal attacks, lies, or divisive rhetoric. Children who watch or overhear these conversations may begin to view shouting, blaming, or hostility as the norm for resolving disagreements rather than engaging in respectful dialogue.

Driving and road rage: A parent or adult who loses control behind the wheel—yelling at other drivers, speeding, or cutting people off—teaches children that aggressive behavior is justified when we're upset. Kids in the back seat of the car often mirror the stress and anger they witness, learning that it's acceptable to lash out when frustrated.

Workplace behavior: Adults who complain about their colleagues or gossip about their coworkers in front of their children send a message that it's OK to disrespect others or speak negatively about people behind their backs. It can normalize unhealthy work attitudes and erode children's understanding of professionalism and kindness in the workplace.

A common response when bullying is called out in adult environments is to minimize it. "They're just having a bad day," "That's just their management style," or "It's tough love," are phrases we often hear when someone crosses the line. In reality, these are excuses, thinly veiled attempts to avoid addressing the toxic behavior head-on.

As parents, we tell our children about the importance of being kind, about the importance of treating one another the way we want to be treated ourselves. Yet, do kids really see this behavior in action? Are we really leading by example? It's important to note that as adults—*all* adults—this is our inherent responsibility, like it or not. And largely, we are not leading by example.

And this is where I started to look—very closely—at the impact Shane's life could have on others. I want to call attention to the words we speak, the behaviors we emulate, and how we are all likely guilty of the "do as I say, not as I do" mentality.

The Universal Thread of Bullying

Bullying is a universal experience, one that we are all connected to in some way. Whether we like to admit it or not, most of us have, at some point, either bullied someone, been bullied, or witnessed bullying in action. Often, it's a combination of these experiences that we carry with us, shaping how we interact with others and view the world around us.

From childhood playgrounds to adulthood, the dynamics of bullying can be found everywhere. It's easy to think of bullying as something that only happens among children, but the reality is that it manifests in different ways throughout life—sometimes, in subtle, passive-aggressive forms, and other times, in blatantly harmful ways. Many of us have been on the receiving end of someone's cruelty, whether it was through harsh words, exclusion, or physical intimidation. But just as often, we have been the ones exerting power over others, perhaps out of fear or insecurity, without realizing the full impact of our actions.

Worse still is the role of the bystander. How many of us have stood idly by, watching someone else being torn down, convinced it wasn't our place to step in? In those moments, our silence can be just as damaging as the bullying itself. Yet, we tell ourselves stories to ease the guilt: "It's not my fight," or "They'll work it out." But the truth is, by doing nothing, we allow the cycle of hurt to continue.

What makes bullying such a powerful force is how common it is and how deeply it affects our emotional lives. The wounds left by bullying—whether we are the victim, the perpetrator, or the witness—can linger for years, shaping how we see ourselves and the world around us. To break free from the hold of these experiences, we have to first recognize their universality and challenge ourselves to do better for the people around us and for ourselves. Only then can we begin to heal and create a world where kindness and empathy take root in place of cruelty and indifference.

Think About It

When I describe bullying as a matter of life or death, I imagine that, for some, this can seem like hyperbole. But I am here to tell you that it most certainly is not. Regardless of your age, role, or title, I wrote this book to (hopefully) help you take a step back and recognize the impact that your words and actions can have on others. Not to sound dramatic, but bullying behavior really does seep into the miniscule pores of every aspect of our society, and it tends to spread like a malignancy, often going unnoticed until it's too late.

When I set out to write this book, I always kept Shane at the front of my mind. What would this sweet person, my son, part of me, part of my soul, want me to convey to anyone reading this book? What would he want his message to be?

Determining that message was really important because, for me to live in truth and embody Shane's core essence, I had to know what he would want me to say, not just as his mother, but by using his voice as a catalyst for change here on earth.

What would he want me to say to *you*, the reader of this book?

I eventually distilled this down to a core message. *Kind really is the new cool.* This may sound trite, but it is not. I hope that by reading this book, you'll have a newfound belief that creating a compassionate culture is the antidote to bullying behavior—of, by, and to people of all ages. It's a solution that has unfortunately been lost somewhere along the way.

Here's what I know. My son was extraordinary. He had a sparkle other people noticed. The kids who bullied him extinguished that flame through their hateful words and actions. I want to light the flame of kindness in us all.

I want us all to be Earth Angels.

Defining an Earth Angel

> *You can easily judge the character of a man by how he treats those who can do nothing for him.*
> *—Johann Wolfgang von Goethe*

An Earth Angel is not someone with wings or a halo, but rather a person who moves quietly through the world, making it better in ways most people never notice. They are the ones who offer comfort in times of distress, lend a hand when no one is looking, and provide support without expectation. Earth Angels don't seek recognition or praise; they simply feel a deep calling to spread kindness and love wherever they go.

What sets an Earth Angel apart is their ability to see beyond the surface. They cut through life's distractions—the noise, the superficial, the ego-driven acts, and instead focus on what truly matters: connection, compassion, and presence. They show up when others disappear, offering calm in the chaos, light in the darkness. It's not always in grand gestures or dramatic moments; often, their influence is felt in the small, quiet acts of generosity that ripple outward, affecting far more than anyone could ever measure.

An Earth Angel understands that life's value is not in what we accumulate or achieve but in how we touch the lives of others. They recognize that we are all connected, and their actions reflect a deep, intuitive knowledge that kindness can be transformative. Their presence reminds us that the world can be a softer, more beautiful place if we choose to live with open hearts and mindful intentions.

Abraham Lincoln is often remembered for his wisdom, humility, and deep sense of kindness, even in the face of great division and conflict. His words and actions reflect a belief in the power of compassion and empathy to heal wounds and unite people.

Lincoln's approach to leadership, especially during the Civil War, was grounded in the idea that understanding and patience were essential to reuniting the country. He often spoke about the importance of looking for the good in others rather than focusing on their faults.

While Lincoln's inaugural addresses don't specifically mention "Earth Angels," his speeches are filled with words of wisdom that reflect the spirit of kindness, unity, and compassion—qualities often associated with the concept of Earth Angels. One powerful quote from his first inaugural address (March 4, 1861) particularly resonates with these ideals:

> *We are not enemies, but friends. We must not be enemies. Though passion may have strained, it must not break our bonds of affection. The mystic chords of memory, stretching from every battlefield and patriot grave to every living heart and hearthstone all over this broad land, will yet swell the chorus of the Union, when again touched, as surely they will be, by the better angels of our nature.*

This passage beautifully speaks to the idea of overcoming division and conflict with compassion, understanding, and our "better angels"—a sentiment that aligns with the notion of Earth Angels who bring peace and healing through their actions. Our "better angel" (i.e., Earth Angel) lives within each of us—our conscience—that element that enables us to know right from wrong and simply yearns to make the world a better place. I wholeheartedly believe that people are not born hateful or bigoted; these are things that are learned. Yet, despite life's experiences, we all have a "better angel" living inside us.

This idea of doing good and putting good out into the world is not new. While I was researching this book, I discovered that the idea of "pay it forward" has its origins in 317 BC in an ancient play in Athens. In more modern times, it was used in Lily Hardy Hammond's book *In the Garden of Delight*, published in 1916. Her famous quote is:

> *I never repaid Great Aunt Letitia's love to her, any more than she repaid her mother's. You don't pay love back; you pay it forward.*

EARTH ANGELS

An Earth Angel encapsulates the spirit of compassion and empathy in a world often overshadowed by darkness and negativity. Earth Angels are individuals who radiate positivity and warmth, offering solace and support to those in need without requiring recognition or reward.

EARTH ANGEL STORY: GRIFFIN AND ROSE

When my son Griffin was in fourth grade, he was given an assignment by his teacher—Mr. Harter at Creekside Elementary School in Danville, California—to perform a random act of kindness for someone and then write about the experience. Mr. Harter's assignment had a positive forever impact on my boys and me. Griffin put a great deal of thought into what he wanted to do for this assignment. One day, we were at the grocery store, and he decided he wanted to give a dozen roses to an elderly woman. At the time, money was really tight because we had just moved—a dozen roses weren't exactly in my budget. But he was so excited about his decision that there was no way I could say no. He carefully selected a bouquet of cream-colored roses wrapped in paper. It was very important to him to not choose just anyone to give them to. He said he "would know" as soon as he saw the right person.

So, we sat in the car and waited. And waited. After about twenty minutes, he spotted an elderly woman grabbing her cart, and he shot up in his seat and said, *"Her!"* So I walked him across the street and stood back and watched as he tapped the woman's back as she was about to enter the store. She was clearly surprised to see a little boy standing there holding up a dozen roses. I watched her look of complete confusion turn to absolute joy as he gave her the flowers. She took the roses and gave him a huge hug. It was a moment I will cherish forever.

CHAPTER ONE

A heartwarming moment captured: Griffin proudly holding his bouquet of roses, ready to spread kindness for his special school assignment—a random act of kindness. His smile reflects the thoughtfulness and excitement he poured into this meaningful gesture, showcasing his big heart and genuine desire to brighten someone's day. This simple yet powerful act serves as a reminder that even small gestures can make a big difference.

Griffin was beaming from ear to ear as he walked to me. He told me that when he explained to the woman about the assignment, she started to cry. As it turned out . . . her name was Rose. Apparently, her husband had recently passed away, and this was her first time going to the grocery store to shop for just one person. It was one of those moments that gives you goosebumps.

It was an Earth Angel moment that I will never forget.

> *It was very important to him to not choose just anyone to give them to. He said he "would know" as soon as he saw the right person.*

23

Earth Angels understand the ripple effect. That one kind action always leads to another. They embrace interconnectedness and recognize that everyone has worth, and they understand the importance of treating others with dignity and respect.

The ripple effect doesn't only apply to kindness and integrity. Negativity and toxic behavior also spread. Toxicity often expands and "infects" others—like a virus. I can remember working for a very toxic boss, and the demands on my time were so intense that I was getting home very late and often working well past my kids' bedtimes. I would come home exhausted (and grouchy), and on the occasions I got home at a reasonable time, I was still working, so my attention wasn't focused on what really mattered—my boys. I was miserable in the job, and even though I never told them what was happening, my sons knew. Kids always know. I didn't have a work-life balance, and consequently, my kids were walking on eggshells when they were around me. I'm haunted by that too.

Earth Angels understand that we are all part of a greater tapestry of life, like a giant quilt.

At its core, being an Earth Angel is not simply things that we do, but who we are. In a world often fraught with turmoil and uncertainty, Earth Angels serve as reminders of the inherent goodness within humanity simply by leading by example.

Lack of compassion and toxic behavior have become a silent epidemic in our society—a plague that is impacting countless people. Toxic behaviors not only cost us our mental health, but they can also act like a parasite and eat away at our self-esteem, confidence, and self-worth. The victims typically lose passion for things they once enjoyed. They leave jobs where they are treated miserably. They retreat from the world when they feel friendless. It affects self-esteem and peace of mind. In short, it impacts people to their core. Imagine if we could simply uplift or inspire people by discovering our unique skills and uncovering our superpowers, or—better yet—enabling others to recognize their own superpowers? Instead of demeaning someone or looking at others as random strangers, what would happen if at least one reader of this book started to look at others as fellow human beings? Just imagine what would be possible.

Think about someone in your life who made you feel truly special. Someone who saw something in you that you couldn't yet see in yourself. Maybe it was a parent, a mentor, a friend, or perhaps a stranger. Whoever they were, they believed in you when you didn't believe in yourself. Their encouragement, their quiet confidence in your abilities likely made you feel like you could move mountains. That feeling—the one where someone truly *sees* you, values you, and makes you feel capable—is a gift few give, but it resonates forever when received. That person, in that moment, was one of your Earth Angels. Each has left a forever positive imprint on you, and you are a better person because of them.

So, I cordially invite you to take this journey with me. When I say, "Be that person," I ask that you try to be the Earth Angel who, like Shane, lights up the room and helps make others believe in humanity again. The person who welcomes the outsiders and embraces diversity. The person who sincerely compliments a stranger and makes their day; the person who listens when someone is having a bad day. Sometimes, in the words of Buddhist scholar Thich Nhat Hanh, all it takes is a smile: "Sometimes your joy is the source of your smile, but sometimes your smile can be the source of your joy."

We can all be that person.
Will you join me?

chapter two
childhood bullying

the scars remain

The two most important days in your life are the day you are born and the day you find out why.
—MARK TWAIN

Bullying can leave scars that never fully heal. Like old wounds, memories can remain dormant for years and resurface when you least expect them through something as simple as a sound, a scent, or a song. Feelings of shame, anger, and isolation may come to the surface again, leaving us to question, "What did I do to deserve this?" The answer, of course, is simple: nothing.

My Bullying Story

Writing this book has been a journey of vulnerability, dredging up memories I'd buried long ago. I prepared myself as best as I could because it is really important that this book come from a place of truth. This particular chapter took me some time to write because it forced me to remember things that I have intentionally suppressed for most of my life.

I was born with strabismus, which made my right eye misalign, resulting in a childhood of corrective surgeries. I don't remember being treated differently, but that changed when I entered fourth grade as the "new kid" in a new school. It's hard enough being the new kid, but it immediately became obvious that there was something different about me. And by this, I don't mean in a gifted way. Think of it like when a pack of lions hunts a group of gazelles. When a slower, older, injured, or baby gazelle becomes separated from the herd, they are the target for attack, and ultimately, the kill. Every day, I sat alone at lunch (I dreaded lunchtime); no one would play with me at recess (I dreaded recess too). Worse, the "cool kids" would dare each other to approach me, pretend to be my friend, and then laugh behind my back. I had always loved going to school. But because of what was happening, I eventually hated going and dreaded Sundays, just knowing I would have to go back the next day. Sadly, I never told anyone about what was happening. I'm ashamed to say that if I had to do it all over again, I would likely still not say anything. Sadly ironic.

I withdrew from things that I once enjoyed, grew very isolated, and felt completely alone. I eventually shut down. As a result, my grades plummeted. I wanted to be invisible—the less likely to draw more attention to myself.

Eventually, I was labeled as having a learning disability. I was placed in special classes, further isolating me. The lone bright spot in my new classroom was one of my teachers. While I can't remember her name, her daily kindness and patience are things I will never forget; after all, here I am enshrining her in this book. She encouraged me, instilled hope, and believed in me. She eventually recognized that I did not have a learning disability—I was broken. Somehow, she was able to figure out that, because of the bullying, I had simply stopped trying.

Thanks to her belief in me, I promised myself that for the rest of my life, I would never stop trying. And I never will. I went on to pursue academic and professional success, motivated partly to prove my bullies wrong and to prove my teacher right. I don't say these things to boast, but to emphasize how different my life could have been had it not been for that teacher. That teacher embodied the title of this book. She was *that* person . . . an Earth Angel who left an indelible imprint on my life.

My family realized the impact bullying had on me and arranged another corrective eye surgery. However, while the procedure helped, the underlying insecurities lingered. For years, I hid my strabismus, mastering techniques to minimize its appearance.

Meanwhile, because my parents were finally able to recognize the bullying I had endured, I was able to start fifth grade at a new school in Ardsley, New York. A fresh start. It's important to mention that I was never bullied or mocked for my eyes again. How I felt about myself was a direct result of my own insecurities, resulting from the scars of having been bullied.

Yet, in adulthood, during an on-camera acting class, the issue resurfaced, painfully reminding me of my younger self, so I sought a specialist in New York City. My fiancé accompanied me, realizing for the first time the depth of my struggle. The doctor made a point of explaining that, for my entire life, I had trained myself to hide the imperfection by simply closing my eyes and looking the other way. When the doctor looked at me and said, "I can help you," I started to cry because I believed him. All of the childhood pain came to the surface, and I felt a gratitude I can never adequately express in words. One thing I will never forget is the doctor telling me, "This is why you are such a humble person. You know what it's like. And that alone is a gift." The doctor's words struck me: My humility was perhaps a gift from years of navigating this imperfection.

For the first time in my life, I really believed that the source of my insecurities would finally be eliminated forever. One week before my surgery, I discovered I was pregnant, and the surgery had to be rescheduled. On April 1, 2003, my son Ryan came into the world.

A mere six weeks later, I had the surgery, and for the first time in my life, I was told it was a success. However, because there was so much scar tissue left from my last surgeries, the surgeon had to align my left eye to my right eye. While both eyes were bandaged, I eventually healed, and I found myself adjusting to a new vision of the world—physically and metaphorically.

Life moved on, and I became a mother. Every experience has shaped me, reminding me that our deepest scars often shape our greatest strengths. The path wasn't easy, but it provided me with resilience and has led me here to write this book.

In truth, I've gone through periods when I've felt like my entire existence was immersed in and defined by the way that I looked and dressed. I believed looking better would alter the way I was seen and treated by the people around me. I recently moved, and one of the things I uncovered was a letter I had written many years ago, which I feel is particularly relevant to this chapter:

CHAPTER TWO

A LETTER TO MY YOUNGER SELF:

You don't know me, but I know you! There are so many things that I wish I could do to stop time, sit with you, and tell you stories of the blessings I've earned and the lessons I've learned the hard way, for these are always the most important.

I would implore that you never forget that life really is short, and how measuring your worth is not based on what you look like or the clothes you wear. I would make you look in the mirror until you truly appreciate, admire, respect, and love the person looking back.

I would tell you that even though you will become very discouraged at times and want to give up, always keep going because every single step you take is one step closer to the woman you will one day become.

I would tell you how glad I am that I don't have to be your age again. But not to worry. Along the way, you will be hurt, healed, embarrassed, proud, scared, brave, sad, happy, insecure, confident, naïve, intuitive. But always be authentic, for it is only when you can be your true self that you can be truly content. Don't be afraid to just be yourself, or you may never discover who you really are.

I would tell you that when you try to look like, act like, be like someone else, the world will never get to know you. Eventually, the real you would be gone forever—and you will become a person you were not meant to be.

I wish I could tell you not to let others' opinions of you matter. I wish I could make you realize that the only opinion of yourself that matters is your own. I wish I could tell you that you will soon understand this. But I can't, because you won't.

I would tell you that "having it all" should never be confused with money or fame. Having it all includes the scars you've earned along the way, the obstacles you've overcome, and the chances you've taken. Having it all is also understanding that you don't fail, you temporarily fall. It's about a slow evolution—so enjoy the ride.

How I wish I could step in and prevent so much of what is yet to come—yet these are the very things that will shape you into the beautiful human being you are. You'll never have it all, but you'll have what you need. Not a single person on earth has it all—even those who try to flaunt that they do, for these are often the people who have the least.

Finally, I'd give you a gigantic hug and make you promise to stop wasting time wanting what you don't have. Cherish what you do have. Always stay in the moment instead of focusing on the next best thing. For this won't allow you to appreciate the things you've already done.

I'm so very proud of you. Now, let's get on to being proud of yourself.

Love,
Me

That insecure, afraid little girl is still very much alive deep inside me, and I have no doubt that, no matter what happens, she will always live within me, and that's OK because I'm proud of her. And every so often, I just want to hug her. I want to tell her everything will be OK. That she will ultimately endure more hardships and pain—but the truth is, no one on earth escapes that; it's simply a part of life. I inherently know, for some reason that I do not yet fully understand, that my past pain must have a purpose. And I have to believe part of that purpose is why I am writing to you, the reader, right now.

Looking back on those formative years, it's clear to me now that we are all just trying to figure out who we are and where we fit in. At that age, we become hyperaware of how others see us—friends, teachers, classmates—and it can feel like everyone is measuring us against invisible standards. Whether it's how we dress, how we look, or how we act, the pressure to conform and fit in is overwhelming. We're constantly trying to find our place, wondering if we're too much of one thing or not enough of another.

In the early years, everyone struggles with insecurities and self-doubt even though it rarely feels that way because we can only see through our own lens. It's easy to believe that we're the only ones who don't quite belong, when in reality, everyone is navigating the same confusing terrain of adolescence, trying to find a balance between being accepted and staying true to ourselves, often unsure of who we even want to be. This journey to figure out where we fit in is one of the most universal parts of growing up—full of missteps, misunderstandings, and moments where we feel utterly lost. But in the end, it's through those moments that we begin to learn more about who we really are and where we truly belong.

I'm left to wonder what my life would have been like had I never been bullied and had we not lost Shane to bullying. I'm pretty sure I would never have had the inspiration to write this book.

It still sucks, though.

JIMMY'S PARTY: A LESSON IN BELONGING

Starting high school was like stepping into an unknown world. I was trying to figure out who I was, where I fit in, and how to mask my insecurities. Every day felt like navigating a sea of unfamiliar faces and unwritten rules. The popular kids seemed to shine effortlessly, while I was quietly trying to find my place. High school is hard enough, let alone when you've had your confidence shattered in the past.

One day, my friends caught wind of a party at Jimmy Plitnick's house. Jimmy was one of the most popular kids in school—a star athlete with a magnetic personality. Everyone wanted to be near him, and the thought of walking into his party made my stomach churn with anxiety. I was convinced that if I showed up, I'd be laughed at, or worse, turned away at the door.

The night of the party arrived, and my girlfriends coaxed me into going. As we approached the house, I could hear the muffled sound of music and laughter spilling out. My heart raced as we walked up the driveway. What was I doing here?

But then something extraordinary happened. The door opened, and there was Jimmy. He greeted us each by name (I couldn't believe he knew my name!) with a big smile and said, "Come on in!" His warmth was genuine, and in that moment, all my fears melted away. Instead of judgment, there was acceptance. Instead of exclusion, there was belonging.

That night, I realized that a single act of kindness could leave a lasting impression. Jimmy could have easily ignored us or dismissed us as unimportant. We all know the cliques of high school. Instead, he genuinely welcomed us into his world without hesitation, and in doing so, he showed me that sometimes the people we think are untouchable are just as capable of lifting others up.

I'll never forget that night, not because of the party itself, but because of how Jimmy made me feel—seen, included, and valued. It was a small moment in his life, but for me, it was monumental. It reminded me how powerful simple actions can be.

Jimmy's welcome became a blueprint for how I wanted to treat others. In a world that can be harsh and unkind, that one moment taught me the extraordinary impact of an ordinary act of kindness.

Cultivating Kindness: A New Cultural Norm

> *What you do makes a difference, and you have to decide what kind of difference you want to make.*
> —Jane Goodall

Imagine a world where kindness is the norm, a world shaped by our everyday actions. It starts with each of us: the compassion we show to a barista after a mistaken order, the understanding we offer a struggling coworker, the patience we extend to our children. Each small act of empathy creates a ripple effect, building toward a culture of respect and compassion. This isn't an impossible dream but a collective effort—a choice we have to actively make moment by moment—to lead with kindness. By living with empathy, we can shift our culture to one where kindness is second nature. Change doesn't happen overnight, but by consciously living with empathy and grace, we can begin to shift the cultural norm, one kind act or word of inspiration at a time.

I hope to spend my life encouraging others to see that this world can be kinder, more compassionate, and more connected. When I speak to kids, I emphasize that happy people are kind, while bullying often comes from pain or unhappiness. It's a message of hope and understanding, reminding them that people who feel good within tend to spread kindness, while those struggling with inner hurt may act out negatively. Kindness, I tell them, is a strength, a reflection of inner peace.

"Hurt people hurt people" can be a tough concept for kids to grasp. It's natural for children to see things in black and white—good people are kind; mean people are bad. The truth, though, is more complex. Helping kids understand that some people act out of their own pain can foster empathy. By teaching them to stand up for themselves while encouraging compassion, we can help them see that kindness can break cycles of pain and anger.

Our society often celebrates self-promotion, but it's time we admire those who lift others up and bring depth and authenticity to the world. Let's shift our focus to the people who make a genuine difference through their kindness and compassion. By valuing substance over image, we can build a culture that finds fulfillment in who we are, not in how we look or how much attention we receive.

Again, every day we are faced with choices. The choices are yours to make.

chapter three
the other *b* words
counteracting bad behavior

Remember there's no such thing as a small act of kindness. Every act creates a ripple effect with no logical end.
—SCOTT ADAMS

We've all encountered bullies in some form—those who tear others down with cruelty, manipulation, or exclusion. But there's another kind of harmful behavior, less obvious but equally damaging—the other *B* words: bitterness, belittling, backstabbing, and betrayal. These actions may not look like traditional bullying, but they chip away at self-worth, confidence, and community. This chapter explores how we can counteract both the overt and subtle forms of bad behavior, focusing on the power of kindness, empathy, and self-awareness. Whether it's standing up to a bully or refusing to engage in gossip, we all have the ability to disrupt the cycle of negativity. It's not always easy, but by choosing better, we set the stage for a healthier, kinder way of living.

After losing Shane, my mind was awash with what seemed like thousands of questions: What signs did I miss? How did this happen? Why did this happen? How could I have saved my son's life? Like the tsunami of grief that I described earlier in the book, I experienced wave upon wave of anguished questions while trying to find answers I inherently knew I'd never find. Yet, for the rest of my life, I will continue to search for them anyway.

Perhaps in order to feel a sense of purpose in my grief, I immersed myself into learning everything I could about bullying. I retreated into my own cocoon and spent countless hours taking online courses, reading journals, memorizing facts, conducting evidence-based research, speaking with bullying experts. It quickly became evident that, for the most part, bullying and cruel behavior is a complex problem that is largely misunderstood and, sadly, far too often ignored.

The fact of the matter is that I had no idea Shane was being bullied. There were no warning signs. As I said in the beginning of the book, if something like this can happen to my family, it can happen to anyone.

Every time I hear of a bullying experience, my heart breaks a little more and I experience a myriad of emotions: empathy, sympathy, sadness, anger, helplessness, hopelessness, grief, and others that are tough to put into words. Through this, I've come to recognize how large the issue is and, as you'll read in chapter seven, how important it is for me to use this knowledge as a superpower. Strength typically requires a certain amount of vulnerability. Believe me when I say that writing this book is the most vulnerable thing I have ever done in my life.

Yet, if opening myself up to being vulnerable through honesty and transparency helps even just one person recognize how important they are, or the impact their behavior and words have on others, or if it inspires just one person to want to be a better human being, then I suppose that telling Shane's story was worth it. I never want to hear another story about someone taking their own life because they feel it's the only way to escape the pain and fear. I never want to hear about another mother having to bury her child because of bullying.

But it goes far beyond that. We each need to act when we see something that we know is inherently wrong.

There were ample opportunities Shane's school ignored. They could have saved his life. Shane's school didn't just miss the warning signs—they ignored the neon signs flashing and begging for help, signs so bright and unmistakable that they should have been impossible to overlook.

Apparently, for months, Shane was searching on the school library's computer for ways to take his own life. Rightly, this search content was flagged each time. Yet, Shane's desperate pleas went unnoticed by those who should have been watching. The digital trail was there, a clear cry for help that no one answered. The school's system flagged these searches, sending multiple notifications, yet not one was opened or addressed. These were more than just missed opportunities; they were glaring signals that Shane was in profound distress, signals that should have triggered intervention, support, and care. Had we known, we could have saved him. Had the school responded to even one of those notifications, Shane's life might have been saved. But instead, those signs went ignored, and we lost Shane to a tragedy that could have been prevented.

The school's inaction and indifference created a void where support should have been, likely leaving Shane feeling trapped and alone. In the end, the system's failure to intervene contributed to the heartbreaking tragedy of Shane taking his own life—a preventable loss had the cries for help been heard and acted upon.

This is yet another thing I will be haunted by for the rest of my life. Shane *never* displayed any warning signs of a child who was being bullied. Until taking my last breath, I will ask myself why he didn't speak up, why he felt that taking his own life was the only way out. Why he didn't love himself as much, or more so, than he was truly loved. Why he couldn't open up to me.

What Exactly Is Bullying?

I want to interject here that this book won't contain a ton of facts and figures because there are already many resources available for that. Having said that, in order to address the core issue at hand, we cannot eradicate bullying until we possess a shared understanding of what bullying behavior is and how to recognize it when it happens.

Bullying is so much more than just hurtful words or physical antagonism—it's a *pattern of behavior* designed to *aggressively* intimidate, control, or belittle another person. Whether it takes the form of verbal abuse, social exclusion, online harassment, or subtle manipulation, bullying thrives on creating an *imbalance of power*. It can happen anywhere—in schools, workplaces, families, and online—and its effects can be deeply damaging, leaving emotional and psychological scars long after the incidents end. Understanding exactly what bullying is, and how it manifests in its many forms, is essential if we are to counteract it with kindness and compassion. This book aims to explore that balance, showing how the power of kindness can challenge and transform bullying behaviors, creating a culture of respect and empathy. There is one thing anyone reading this book should understand: Bullying behavior—regardless of age, situation, or location—is abuse.

This is worth repeating: Bullying behavior is *abuse*.

According to the National Institutes of Health:

> *Bullying is unwanted aggressive behavior by another person or group of people. In bullying, there is always an actual or perceived power imbalance, and the aggression is repeated multiple times or is highly likely to be repeated. Bullying also includes cyberbullying, a type of aggression that is carried out through electronic means, such as through the internet, email, or mobile devices. People of all ages can be bullied, and bullying may take place at home, school, or work. Because of cyberbullying, bullying can occur almost anywhere at any time.*[2]

Turning a Blind Eye: The Modern Face of Bullying

The word *bully* often conjures up childhood images—playground taunts, stolen lunch money, or exclusion from games. This outdated image is exactly why so many adults fail to recognize bullying behavior when it happens. This outdated view blinds them to the more subtle, nuanced forms of adult bullying that exist in social circles, online interactions, and even family dynamics. Whether it's passive-aggressive comments, social manipulation, gaslighting, or digital harassment, these forms of bullying are often downplayed or dismissed because they don't fit the traditional mold. Adults may see these behaviors

---

[2] "Bullying," *National Institute of Child Health and Human Development*, last modified September 1, 2023, https://www.nichd.nih.gov/health/topics/factsheets/bullying#:~:text=Bullying%20is%20unwanted%20aggressive%20behavior,highly%20likely%20to%20be%20repeated.

as minor conflicts or personality clashes, not recognizing the lasting emotional and psychological harm they can cause. By holding on to outdated ideas of what bullying looks like, society misses the pervasive and damaging nature of bullying, allowing toxic behaviors to flourish in various settings without being challenged or addressed. The modern, specifically adult, bully is not a playground tormentor; they are often more subtle, sophisticated, and harder to identify.

As I've mentioned, I want this book to focus more on positivity and stories of people who embody Earth Angels. I want to give the bad behavior less air, perhaps that will help to extinguish it or push it down deep into that dark abyss so that we can begin to see bullying behavior as the exception, not the norm. Let's instead give the air to the beautiful angels, the Earth Angels.

In 2023, Paul Rudd demonstrated a beautiful act of kindness when he reached out to a twelve-year-old boy named Brody Ridder, who had been experiencing bullying at school. Brody's mother had shared a heartbreaking story about how her son had only received a few signatures in his yearbook, despite asking his classmates. Feeling rejected, Brody had written in his own yearbook, "I hope you make some more friends."

When Paul Rudd heard about the story, he decided to reach out personally. He sent Brody a handwritten note, offering support and encouragement. In his letter, Rudd wrote, "It's important to remember that even when life is tough that things get better. There are so many people that love you and think you're the coolest kid there is." Along with the letter, Rudd also sent Brody an autographed Ant-Man helmet, making it clear that he saw him as a hero in his own right.[3]

---

3   Rachel Paula Abrahamson, "Mom Shares How Paul Rudd Comforted Bullied Son After No One Signed His Yearbook: 'So many people love you'," *Today*, July 7, 2022, https://www.today.com/parents/parents/mom-shares-paul-rudd-comforted-bullied-son-no-one-signed-yearbook-rcna37073.

CHAPTER THREE

This simple but powerful gesture was a reminder of how kindness and compassion can help counteract the effects of bullying. Rudd's thoughtful response likely made a world of difference to Brody, showing him that he was valued and seen, even when others failed to acknowledge him.

John Cena has become a powerful symbol of kindness through his extraordinary work with the Make-A-Wish Foundation. He holds the record for the most wishes granted by a single individual, with over 650 wishes fulfilled for children facing critical illnesses. Cena's commitment to the foundation goes beyond just appearances; he takes the time to personally connect with each child, offering them hope, joy, and unforgettable memories during some of the toughest moments of their lives.[4]

Cena treats each wish with deep sincerity, often visiting children in hospitals, attending their birthday parties, or welcoming them to WWE events. He's known for his genuine interactions—taking photos, signing autographs, and spending quality time to make sure each child feels special and seen. Cena has said that he never turns down a Make-A-Wish request, showing his dedication to brightening the lives of children who are going through unimaginable challenges.

By consistently showing up and giving his time, Cena models the power of kindness and compassion. His work with Make-A-Wish reminds us that even small gestures of love and attention can make a lasting impact on those who need it most. An Earth Angel.

As I reflect on everything we've explored so far, one thing is clear: There are Earth Angels all around us. They're the ones who quietly spread kindness, offer support, and lift us up when we need it most. We just need to open our eyes and amplify their light instead of giving

---

4   Zoe Sottile, "John Cena Breaks Make-A-Wish Record with 650 Wishes Granted," *CNN*, September 24, 2022, https://www.cnn.com/2022/09/24/us/john-cena-make-a-wish-record/index.html.

our attention to the other *B* words: bitterness, belittling, betrayal, and so on. By choosing to celebrate and elevate the good in others, we create a ripple effect that changes the world for the better. The more we recognize and nurture the Earth Angels among us, the more we'll find ourselves surrounded by kindness, compassion, and love.

The Digital Battlefield: Tackling Cyberbullying

In today's world, bullying has found a new and often more insidious platform: the internet. Cyberbullying can be relentless, spreading beyond the walls of schools or workplaces and following people into their most personal spaces. Unlike face-to-face bullying, the online world allows "bashing" (another *B* word): harmful words and actions to be amplified and seen by countless others, often without consequence for the bully. For victims, this can feel overwhelming, as the hurt doesn't stop when the day ends—it lingers, accessible at any moment with just a tap or click.

Alarmingly, among children and teens, the figures are utterly devastating—59 percent of US teenagers have experienced bullying or harassment online, and 14.5 percent of children between the ages of nine and twelve have been cyberbullied.[5]

This concept is so important that I'll be dedicating an entire chapter to it that dives into the rise of online bullying, how it affects not just kids but adults as well, and the unique challenges it presents. We'll explore how the anonymity of the internet fuels cruelty, the lasting emotional damage it can cause, and—most importantly—how we can combat it with empathy, awareness, and action. Just as we

---

[5] Ivana Vojinovic, "Heart-Breaking Cyberbullying Statistics," *DataProt*, May 5, 2023, accessed December 1, 2023, https://dataprot.net/statistics/cyberbullying-statistics/.

counteract bullies in real life, we must learn to confront cyberbullying with strength, kindness, and a shared responsibility to make online spaces safer for everyone.

The Invisible Force: Workplace Bullying and Toxic Culture

Workplace bullying is often an invisible force woven into the fabric of office culture, and it can have a profound impact on both individuals and entire organizations. Unlike schoolyard bullying, it's rarely out in the open. Instead, it hides behind passive-aggressive comments, exclusion, undermining, and manipulation. This toxic behavior can poison a work environment, creating a culture where fear, anxiety, and distrust thrive. Employees who experience this form of bullying may suffer in silence, unsure of how to confront it or if it's even safe to speak up. In this part of the chapter, we'll dive into the subtle ways workplace bullying manifests, how it erodes morale and productivity, and most importantly, what can be done to change the culture. By recognizing the invisible forces at play, we can begin to dismantle them and rebuild workplaces rooted in respect, collaboration, and kindness.

Culture is the invisible hand that guides the everyday interactions in any workplace. While leaders set the tone, it's the collective actions of everyone within the organization that truly define it. The small, seemingly insignificant moments of kindness—or cruelty—can change the trajectory of an entire team. Workplace culture is not static; it's fluid and constantly shaped by our interactions, good or bad.

Bullying in the workplace is often dismissed as isolated incidents, but its effects are rarely confined to one person. A single act of bullying, whether it's exclusion, belittling, or undermining, sets off a chain reaction. The initial victim suffers, but so do the bystanders who witness it. And, as I mentioned earlier when I was working in my own toxic environment, their families. In every workplace, the behaviors we exhibit, whether kind or cruel, carry a ripple effect. Just as a single stone creates expanding circles when thrown into a pond, our words, actions, and attitudes spread far beyond their immediate target. Bullying erodes a company's foundation, sending waves of fear, resentment, and disengagement. Morale plummets and a culture of fear is created. Over time, this ripple turns into a wave that can lead to lower productivity, higher turnover, and long-term damage to the organization's foundation (and reputation).

On the other hand, just as negativity can spread, so too can positivity. Acts of kindness can lift morale, boost productivity, and foster trust, creating their own ripple effect to create a culture of respect and collaboration. When employees feel valued and motivated, even by something like a simple "thank you," an encouraging word, or stepping in to support a colleague, trust and camaraderie build.

Leaders play a pivotal role in amplifying or dampening these ripples. When managers allow bullying to go unchecked, they are complicit in its spread. Conversely, leaders who actively promote kindness and address toxicity head-on become the champions of positive culture.

Recovering from a culture of bullying is difficult, but not impossible. Every person, no matter their role, has the power to create ripples in the workplace. The decisions we make—whether to stand by or step in, to tear down or lift up—shape the environment we work in.

A Responsibility We All Share: Recognizing Cruelty When We See It

Bullying doesn't stop when we grow up. It just takes on different forms. Adult bullying is more subtle, but equally harmful, and it often goes unnoticed or is dismissed as part of being an adult. The challenge is that adult bullying is often harder to identify. Unlike the schoolyard taunts or overt physical aggression that we associate with childhood bullying, adult bullying can take on more insidious forms: gossiping to undermine someone's reputation, passive-aggressive comments that chip away at confidence, or exclusion from social or professional circles. In these moments, it becomes all too easy to dismiss such behavior as mere personality conflicts or minor disagreements, allowing toxic patterns to continue unchecked.

This part of the chapter explores how to recognize adult bullying when we see it, often disguised as "harmless banter" or "tough love." These behaviors may seem less obvious, but their effects are real and deeply felt. Understanding what bullying looks like in adulthood is the first step toward breaking the cycle and fostering a more supportive, empathetic environment in all areas of our lives. Adult bullying can take many forms, and its impact on self-worth, confidence, and emotional well-being is often profound, especially because it's so hard to recognize and confront. I've seen it happen, and the effects are real and lasting.

One of my close friends experienced bullying in the workplace that completely eroded her sense of self. She was working hard to prove herself in a competitive environment, but there was one colleague who always found a way to undercut her efforts. In meetings, this person would make dismissive comments about her contributions, often with a sarcastic smile or under the guise of humor. It seemed minor at first, just a few offhand remarks, but it became a pattern. My friend started to question her abilities, overthinking every decision she made, constantly worrying that she was falling short. Over time, she became withdrawn, no longer speaking up in meetings or sharing her ideas, afraid they'd be shot down. This experience damaged her confidence deeply, and even after she left that job, she carried those doubts with her, questioning her worth in future roles.

Another personal story involves someone I knew who was slowly isolated by a group of friends. It wasn't the direct name-calling or confrontation we associate with bullying; it was much quieter. She noticed she was being left out of plans, finding out about gatherings through social media or in passing conversations long after the events had happened. When she asked about it, the excuses were always casual, dismissing her feelings as if she were being too sensitive or overthinking things. But the exclusion took a toll on her. She started questioning whether she was likable, wondering if she had done something wrong. The gradual alienation ate away at her self-esteem, leaving her to internalize the message that she wasn't wanted. The emotional impact was long-lasting, as she became hesitant to trust new friendships, always fearing she would be left out again. It turned out that the reason she was excluded was because she had become separated from her husband. Since she was now single, she was no longer "one of them" and was alienated.

I have personally experienced the effects of adult bullying through subtle undermining and exclusion in professional settings. I remember a time when a group of colleagues consistently left me out of important conversations or decision-making, making me feel like an outsider. It was never direct or hostile, but the isolation was clear, and over time, I started doubting my own value and ability to contribute. I questioned whether I was truly part of the team, and it affected my willingness to speak up or share ideas. The experience lingered long after, as I found myself hesitating in future roles, wondering if I really belonged.

These examples serve as reminders that adult bullying is often a matter of erosion—small, daily actions that chip away at someone's self-worth. As adults, we have the power to stop this erosion by recognizing and addressing toxic behaviors when we see them, whether they happen to us or someone else. Silence and inaction only allow these behaviors to fester, spreading negativity and harm throughout our relationships and environments. We need to be more attuned to the signs, even when they appear in less obvious forms, and take active steps to call them out and create spaces where kindness and respect are the norm, not the exception.

chapter four

the call to lead by example

are you an earth angel?

If you want your children to turn out well, spend twice as much time with them, and half as much money.
—ABIGAIL VAN BUREN, "DEAR ABBY"

Imagine a world where every action, every gesture, and every decision we make echoes far beyond our own lives. This world is not distant or unattainable—it's here, within reach, created by individuals who choose to lead by example.

Leadership transcends traditional settings such as the boardroom or the battlefield. Leaders are found in everyday life, influencing others through their actions, big or small, good or bad.

We often hear about superheroes who swoop in to save the day, but what if the true heroes are those who walk among us daily, making small yet significant choices and performing actions that leave a lasting impact on the people they touch? These are the *Earth Angels*—people like you and me, given the choice to transform the world, one compassionate act at a time.

Every day, we are faced with choices, many of which seem small or inconsequential in the moment. Yet, it's the decisions we make when faced with these choices that define who we are. From the way we respond to a rude remark or comment, to whether we offer help to someone in need, each moment presents an opportunity to lead by example, or not. It's easy to overlook the significance of these choices, but they are the building blocks of character. Each act of kindness, integrity, or patience shapes not only our lives but the lives of those around us. When we choose to lead by example, we show others that compassion, resilience, and empathy are more than ideals, they are actions that can be practiced every single day.

Are you leading by example?

This question is not meant to challenge or confront, but to inspire. In a time when the world can feel disconnected, chaotic, and uncertain, the power to lead lies not in grand gestures but in quiet, consistent actions that reflect the kind of world we want to live in.

When we lead by example, we embody the change we wish to see. We become models of kindness, empathy, and resilience, demonstrating that the path to a better world starts not with someone else, but with ourselves. Every moment is a choice: to lift someone up when they are down or to inspire them by simply being true to the values we hold dear.

In this book, we explore the journey of becoming an Earth Angel, a journey that begins with a simple reflection: How are you leading by example?

From the smallest acts of kindness to the most profound expressions of selflessness, Earth Angels are everywhere. They may not wear wings, but their hearts soar as they lift the spirits of those around them. Their purpose is to inspire, not through words alone, but through actions that leave an indelible mark on others.

As we embark on this exploration, take a moment to reflect on your own life. Who are the Earth Angels who have guided and shaped you? How have their actions, more than their words, changed the course of your journey? And more importantly, how are you walking that path for others?

Leading by example requires time, attention, and awareness. Every encounter we have with others is an opportunity. Did you leave the encounter having left a positive or a negative impact? Did you give something or take something? Were you a positive or a negative influence? Did you help, or did you hurt?

My First Leaders: How My Parents Paved the Way as Earth Angels

> *My own mother and father sacrificed so much to raise my brother and me, and they taught us life's most important lessons in the process often by example. They're my superheroes.*
> —Michael Uslan

The saying "The apple doesn't fall far from the tree" carries both truth and falsity. On the one hand, it's true that many of our values, behaviors, and habits are shaped by our upbringing, with children often mirroring the actions and attitudes of their parents. However, on the other hand, this notion oversimplifies human individuality.

While we may be influenced by those who raised us, we each have the capacity to forge our own path, adopt new perspectives, and break away from patterns that don't serve us—even those we learned from the people who have served as role models throughout our lives. The apple may be shaped by the tree, but it ultimately decides where it will take root.

My mom and dad divorced when I was seven; it wasn't the chaotic, bitter event that so many imagine. In retrospect, it was confusing for me because they never fought. There were never raised voices, no harsh words, just an overwhelming sense of calm. Even after their separation, they remained good friends, a bond they carried until the day my dad passed away. Their respect for one another never wavered, and it was a quiet lesson for me in what true maturity and love can look like, even when a relationship changes. Their example taught me that kindness and mutual respect could transcend any situation.

In the process of writing this book, I started to recognize the powerful lessons my parents (and this includes my stepfather, Roy, as you will soon see as well) have taught me, and the immense impact these lessons have had on my life. Their patience, love, and guidance exemplify what it means to lead by example.

My mom married Roy when I was nine. It could have been a time of transition and tension, especially given what I had gone through in fourth grade, but instead, they worked seamlessly with my dad, communicating openly and ensuring my brother and I never felt torn between them. It wasn't just about getting along; they genuinely cared for one another's well-being and showed us what it meant to be a united front in the face of change. Whether it was making decisions about school, health, or family gatherings, the three of them approached everything as a cohesive unit. Their teamwork and respect for each other made a lasting impact, showing me that family is about love, respect, and always putting the needs of those you care about first.

Roy as a Leader

Roy stepped into our lives with a love and acceptance that made it feel seamless. He has always treated my brother and I as his own, never making us feel like anything less than his blood family. There was no dysfunction, no awkwardness—just a sense of stability and care.

Roy continues to lead by example through his sincere kindness, a quality that shines through in everything he does. He has an incredible ability to make any situation better, no matter how difficult, with his unique sense of humor. It's his way of reminding everyone that life's challenges don't have to be taken too seriously. His humor isn't just about making people laugh—it's about creating an environment of warmth and ease. Roy's kindness runs deep, and his laughter brings people together in a way that only he can. Through both his actions and his humor, he has always shown me what it means to lead with kindness and how a little laughter could go a long way in making life's hardest moments feel a whole lot lighter.

The bond between Shane and his grandpa was as strong and genuine as it gets. Despite not being related by blood, the connection they shared was undeniable. Roy wasn't just a father figure to Shane; he was his confidant, mentor, and role model. Shane looked up to Roy in so many ways, admiring his strength, wisdom, and the way he could bring humor to any situation. In return, Roy saw in Shane a kindred spirit, someone who shared his values of kindness, loyalty, and selflessness.

EARTH ANGELS

Shane and his grandpa Roy. They had a very special relationship.

I loved to be with Grandpa,
his steps were slow like mine;
He never said to "hurry up,"
we always took our time.

Most people have to rush things,
they never stop to see;
Most people don't experience
a bond like you and me.

We created such great memories,
to be cherished in our hearts;
it's something that we'll always have,
even if we are apart.

CHAPTER FOUR

So with every year that passes,
you're no less special than before;
Through every stage and every age,
I'll love you even more.

Right from the very beginning
I knew it right away;
the bond that we created,
was in our hearts to stay.

All I ask, is don't forget me,
whatever that you do;
I'll always be your buddy,
and I'll always be with you.

    Shane and Roy's relationship was built on trust and respect, but what made it even more special was how effortlessly they could enjoy each other's company. Whether it was taking a ride in Roy's T-Bird, sharing a laugh, or just spending quiet moments together, their bond felt more like that of close friends rather than just family. Roy's guidance and presence in Shane's life left a lasting imprint, and Shane, with his kind heart and thoughtful nature, gave Roy a sense of pride and fulfillment in being a grandpa. Their connection was the kind of bond that many only dream of—a perfect blend of love, respect, and shared joy.
    It's very hard to put into words how Roy has impacted not only Shane's life but also the lives of his own children, my mom, and my brother and me (and anyone who has ever known him).

My Father as a Leader

My dad's humility and integrity were values instilled in me from the day I was born. He never sought the spotlight or craved recognition, but he lived his life with an unwavering sense of honesty and quiet strength. His humility was evident in the way he treated everyone with respect, no matter who they were, and he always remained grounded, no matter what life threw at him. Integrity wasn't just something he preached; it was the foundation of how he lived, always doing the right thing, even when no one was watching. Growing up, I witnessed firsthand how these values guided his decisions and shaped his interactions, and they naturally became part of who I am. His example taught me that true character comes from humility and integrity, and those qualities have been a constant compass in my own life, influencing everything I do.

I was twenty-six when my dad passed away, and on that day, I truly felt like I grew up. His presence had always been my anchor, and suddenly, I was faced with the reality of moving forward without him. My dad exemplified what it means to be "the salt of the earth"—a man of quiet strength, unwavering kindness, and genuine goodness. He wasn't just a father; he was my role model, the person whose actions spoke louder than words and whose life was a testament to hard work, honesty, and love. His passing marked a turning point for me, but the lessons he left behind continue to guide me every day.

I'm acutely aware that my dad's values didn't just shape who I am, they've also been deeply instilled in the way I raise my boys. The lessons of integrity, humility, and kindness that he lived by are the same principles I try to pass on to them every day. I find myself teaching them the importance of being honest, of working hard without expecting praise, and of treating others with respect, just as

CHAPTER FOUR

my dad taught me. His influence reaches beyond my own life, and I see his values reflected in the way my boys approach the world. Whether it's in how they show kindness to others or their sense of responsibility, I know that the legacy of my dad's character is being carried on through them. It's one of the greatest honors of my life to raise them with the same love and guidance that he gave me.

My dad had the kind of presence that made people take notice; he looked like a movie star. But beyond his looks, he possessed a natural athletic ability that set him apart. He played semiprofessional baseball, showcasing his skills and passion for the game, and also raced stock cars at the Danbury Racearena in Danbury, Connecticut. He is actually listed as one of the greatest drivers at that track, which is now the Danbury Fair mall. My strabismus affected my depth perception and hand–eye coordination, so it was impossible for me to follow in my dad's athletic footsteps, but his gift was clearly passed down to my son Griffin. I love knowing that a part of my dad's legacy lives on so vibrantly in him.

My dad in his race car at the Danbury Racearena.

Griffin has loved baseball since before he could walk or talk. When he was in kindergarten, he was placed on a team with older kids. In fact, he was so little, his feet couldn't reach the ground when he sat on the bench. One day, after one of his games, one of the parents walked up to him and said, "Great game, Griffin. You played really great today!" to which Griffin replied, "I know."

It took a moment for his comment to register in my brain (what mom hasn't done a double take once or twice over things our kids have said). However, when it did, I stopped in my tracks and pivoted to face him. He stared up at me, not understanding why I looked so genuinely upset (a.k.a. mad). I knew that this was going to be an important life lesson for him, so it was really important that I got it right. I kneeled down to be face-to-face with him and told him about the importance of showing sincere gratitude when someone compliments him. I let him know that his response wasn't appropriate and reminded him that I was raising him (and his brothers) to be good human beings. I told him that his response wasn't OK because it sounded conceited, and I reminded him that no matter how good he may be, it's important to remember to always be humble, and that "he puts on his pants the same way everyone else does" (something I learned from my dad). I told him that he should be very proud of himself for working so hard and practicing. But when someone compliments him, he should always exude gratitude and humility. I then instructed him to go back to the man, to look him in the eyes, shake his hand, and sincerely say, "Thank you."

He refused.

So, I sat on the ground and made it clear that if he did not do what I asked, I would sit there for the rest of the day. It took some time, but I think he really believed we would be sitting there all day (and quite frankly, I was willing to sit there a long time). Finally, he rolled his eyes, and I watched as he approached the gentleman, tapped him on the back and shook his hand. When I saw the way the man responded, I knew I had done the right thing. I told Griffin how proud I was of him and made him promise that he would never take his gifts for granted. To date, he hasn't.

That day, I realized how much my dad led by example. He would have done the same thing to me had I been in the same situation. And now, as Griffin is becoming a man, I know my dad is looking down from heaven with pride.

Just like my dad, my son Ryan has an innate gentleness and a heart full of compassion. He approaches others with empathy, always ready to lend a helping hand or offer a kind word, much like my dad did. There's a quiet strength in the way Ryan carries himself, a grace that makes him stand out, not for attention, but for the genuine care he shows to others. Seeing my dad's kindness reflected so clearly in Ryan is a beautiful reminder of the legacy of love and warmth that lives on through him.

Ryan exhibits kindness and empathy in so many ways every day, just like my dad did. He's the type of person who instinctively checks in on friends who seem a little off, always making sure they feel seen and supported. If someone is left out or struggling, Ryan is the first to invite them in or offer a comforting word. Whether it's helping a younger classmate with their homework, sharing whatever he has without hesitation, or simply being a patient listener when someone needs to talk, Ryan mirrors the quiet strength and compassion my dad showed throughout his life. He has a natural ability to make others feel valued, and it's in these everyday moments that I see my dad's heart and kindness living on through him.

One of the things that gets me through each day is knowing that my dad is looking down on Ryan too, and I must believe he beams with pride witnessing from heaven the genuinely good human being Ryan is.

My heart bursts with pride seeing my dad living through my sons.

When my dad died, I was listed as his next of kin, so it was my responsibility to sign the papers to donate his organs (a process I now sadly know far too well). Because my dad's cancer had spread throughout his entire system, the only viable donations were the retinas in his eyes. When he died, he helped others see.

Trust me, this is yet another irony that will never go unnoticed.

My Mother as a Leader

My mom's cooking has always been about more than just food—it's been a symbol of love, and that love has woven itself into every cherished memory my boys have had with her. Every dish she makes carries with it a fond memory. From the smell of her kitchen to the familiar tastes of her signature meals, her food has a way of bringing the family together, making everyone feel safe, loved, and cared for.

For my boys, each meal is a piece of their childhood they hold close to their hearts. Whether it's "butterfly" cookies or the elaborate holiday feasts, her cooking has become synonymous with comfort and love. They've grown up knowing that her food is an expression of her affection for them, and even the simplest dishes are treasured because of the heart she puts into them. It's not just about the taste—it's about the memories they've made around her table, the laughter, the stories, and the feeling of being surrounded by family. Her cooking is love, and my boys will carry that with them always.

My mom's perseverance is one of the primary reasons I am writing this book. She taught me, through example, that the true meaning of perseverance is not just through words, but by living a life that exemplifies it. Whether it was navigating the complexities of her career, balancing family life, or handling difficulty, she always pushed through with grace. Watching her resilience showed me that perseverance isn't just about surviving difficult times; it's about facing them head-on and refusing to give up.

My first job out of college was working for a large advertising agency in Manhattan. I left for work in the dark and got home in the dark, the constant grind wearing me down day by day. The pressure was immense, and I was so stressed that my mom was genuinely convinced I would drop dead from exhaustion. She could sense how much I needed a break before I completely burned out, and she decided to book a family trip to Club Med in Cancún—a complete getaway from the chaos of Manhattan and my demanding job. It was exactly what I needed: a chance to reset, recharge, and get some much-needed perspective on what really mattered. That trip was a turning point, life-changing. My mom's decision to whisk me away to Cancún was her way of saving me, but it gave me a new perspective with balance and clarity.

I was only twenty-one and had been caught in the grind of the Manhattan rat race, stressed and exhausted, not mature enough to figure out what I truly wanted. That week in Cancún gave me a goal I didn't even know I was searching for. The vibrant, carefree atmosphere at Club Med was a world apart from the stressful hustle I had left behind in New York. I quickly realized that *this* was where I needed to be.

In Club Med terminology, a G.O stands for *gentil organisateur,* which translates to "gracious organizer" in English. G.Os are the staff members who interact with guests, organizing activities, entertainment, and various events to create a fun, social atmosphere. They play a unique role, as they are both hosts and entertainers, responsible for engaging with guests to ensure they have a memorable experience.

From the second I got off the bus as we arrived, I was determined to work for Club Med. They have "villages" (at Club Med, each location is called a village) all over the world, and I didn't care where I went, but I was determined to become a G.O. I was fascinated by their lifestyle and how different it was from my reality back home. They all seemed to be living their best lives, meeting new people from all over the world, and embracing new experiences every day. It wasn't just a vacation; it was a revelation. That week, I saw a life centered around adventure, connection, and happiness. It became clear that I needed to make a change, and that decision started with that one unforgettable trip.

One of the unexpected benefits of taking French since seventh grade was that, at the time, it was a requirement to speak French in order to work for Club Med. This language skill opened a door I didn't even know existed. As soon as I got home and back to work, I went to the art department where my buddies worked and explained the situation. They told me to bring in my résumé and any photos I had taken on the trip, which I did, and they would let me know when "it" was ready.

A few days later, they told me "it" was ready. When I walked in, I was stunned—"it" was a life-size cardboard stand-up of me! On the back, my résumé and the photos from my trip were embossed, making it both eye-catching and unforgettable. It was such a creative, bold way to present myself, and I knew that this was my ticket to standing out. That life-size creation wasn't just a résumé; it was my first real step toward leaving the corporate rat race and heading into a new world of adventure and possibility.

At the time, Club Med's headquarters were just a few blocks away from my office, so I wrapped "it" up and sent "it" via bike messenger, hoping this unconventional approach would catch their attention. A few days later, my gamble paid off when I received an invitation to an interview.

When the day of the interview came, I was both excited and nervous. As I walked to the Club Med office, my nerves kicked in—full force. My hands were shaking so badly I had to stuff them into my pockets just to keep it together. It was such a surreal moment knowing that what happened in the next hour was going to be a turning point in my life. The excitement of what was possible, combined with the fear of the unknown, made that moment unforgettable.

As soon as I walked through the door, I was greeted by a man who exclaimed, "The poster girl! Come in!" My heart raced as I realized that my life-size cardboard résumé had made an impression. That single greeting put me at ease, instantly breaking the ice. All the nervousness I'd felt walking into that office melted away, and I felt a surge of confidence. The unconventional approach had paid off, and it seemed like they were as excited to meet me as I was to be there. From that moment on, I knew that this was the beginning of something truly special.

A few days later I received a call. I was hired. And then it became real.

My first assigned village was in Martinique. It would certainly be the farthest I had ever been from home.

When I arrived, I was full of anticipation. However, it didn't take long for me to realize that the French I had learned in school was nothing like the conversational French needed to communicate with the guests. My job was to greet people, show them around, and explain things to them, but I was completely overwhelmed. I was a world away from home, scared, and unsure of how to fit in or navigate the language barrier. Each day, I felt more out of place, struggling to understand and be understood, and my confidence was plummeting. I was in way over my head, and I knew it.

The excitement I had initially felt about starting this new chapter quickly faded as I struggled to adjust to the language, the culture, and being so far from home. After a particularly tough day, I reached my breaking point and called my mom in tears, telling her that I wanted to come home. I expected her to tell me to book a flight home, but instead, her response caught me by surprise.

She said, "We'll come get you. Just let us know the flight and time." Hearing those words brought a wave of relief, knowing she was ready to bring me back, no questions asked. But then she added something that changed everything: "But maybe if you try to stick it out, you'll have new experiences, make new friends, and have stories to tell for a lifetime."

Her words gave me a moment's pause. She wasn't pushing me to stay, but she was encouraging me to persevere and see the possibilities beyond my fear and discomfort. It was a gentle nudge to be brave, to face the unknown, and to trust that something good might come from the struggle.

I (hesitantly) decided to try to stick it out for as long as I could.

Later that week, I was having a really bad day. I was butchering the language, and, with good reason, people were getting frustrated with me. An elderly couple from France noticed my struggle. The wife saw the anxiety (let's be honest, they were tears) in my eyes and took the time to offer me advice that has stayed with me ever since. She told me, "Learn one word a day, one sentence a week. All people need to know is that you are trying." It was simple but powerful. In that moment, her words shifted everything for me. Rather than focusing on what I couldn't do, I began to focus on what I could—making small, consistent efforts to improve.

She also gifted me an icebreaker that became my lifeline. Sensing my anxiety and desire to connect, she told me, with a playful smile, that humor could be my best ally. She taught me a phrase in French that I wrote out phonetically and quickly memorized by heart:

"*Veuillez excuser mon français. Je parle français comme une vache espagnole, mais j'essaie.*"

"Please excuse my French. I speak French like a Spanish cow, but I'm trying."

The moment she explained it, I laughed, and she reassured me that using humor would show people that I was trying, even if I wasn't perfect. It was lighthearted, self-deprecating, and just the icebreaker I needed to bridge the gap between my nervousness and their understanding. The first time I used it, the tension melted away as people laughed warmly and immediately softened toward me.

Her kindness in teaching me that phrase was about more than just the words; it was about breaking down barriers with humor and vulnerability (like Roy). That simple saying gave me the confidence to engage with others, reminding me that people appreciate the effort and that laughter is a universal language that can ease any situation. It's advice I still carry to this day: Sometimes, the best way to connect is by showing that you're human, trying, and willing to laugh at yourself along the way.

That stranger's kindness not only helped me survive in a foreign place but also gave me a tool to thrive. With each word I learned, my confidence grew, and little by little, I found myself fitting in. Her advice taught me that effort matters more than perfection, and it's a lesson I carry with me to this day. It reminds me that, even in overwhelming situations, taking small steps and showing that you're trying—you're human—can make all the difference.

It was an Earth Angel moment of unexpected connection, reminding me that no matter where we are in the world, humility and kindness have the power to heal and uplift.

Within three weeks I was fluent.

Deciding to persevere and continue working for Club Med turned out to be one of the best decisions of my life. In those moments when I wanted to give up and go home, I never could have imagined that sticking it out would lead to some of the most incredible experiences I've ever had. Staying allowed me to live and immerse myself in other cultures, seeing the world from entirely new perspectives.

But beyond the experiences, the friendships I made are what truly stand out. These weren't just casual acquaintances. I have formed deep, lifelong bonds with people from all corners of the globe (we are called "Soul Family"—more of my Earth Angels). We continue to share laughter, stories, and adventures, and even through tough times (such as when we lost Shane), we grow together through the shared bond of all having worked in such a unique environment. These friendships have become my support system and my family away from home to this day.

It would have been so easy for me to book a flight home and leave behind the discomfort and challenges I was facing. The temptation to return to the safety and familiarity of home was strong, but my mom's words of wisdom and the way she led by example through her own perseverance got me through. Her encouragement to stick it out and see what might unfold gave me the strength to stay, even when I was convinced I couldn't. Her reminder that pushing through hard times could lead to new experiences, friendships, and stories for a lifetime was exactly what I needed to hear, even though it wasn't what I wanted to hear at the time. By following her example, I not only grew as a person, but I also discovered a world full of adventure and connection that I would have missed had I simply given up. That decision, inspired by my mom's resilience, has shaped the course of my life in ways I will always be grateful for. An Earth Angel.

Leaders in the Workforce

> *A true leader is not the one with the most followers, but the one who creates the most leaders.*
> —Neale Donald Walsch

Bob Brunner, my first mentor, was a guiding light who shaped not only my career but also my entire approach to leadership. From the moment I met him, he led by example, showing me that true leadership wasn't about authority or control—it was about trust, transparency, and, most importantly, kindness. Bob believed in empowering others by trusting their abilities, and he taught me that the foundation of any successful team was built on honesty and open communication. He wasn't the kind of leader who ruled with an iron fist; instead, he led with a genuine compassion for those around him, always seeking to uplift and encourage.

Through his mentorship, I learned that leadership is more about the relationships you build than the titles you hold. He showed me how to create an environment where people feel valued and respected, which fosters loyalty and collaboration. Bob's influence taught me to lead with integrity, always being transparent with those I work with and never forgetting the human aspect of a working environment.

His kindness wasn't just a professional trait—it was who he was as a person, and it's the kind of leadership I strive to practice to this day.

After Bob's sudden passing, I found myself at a significant crossroads in my career. His absence left a void that was both personal and professional, and I felt adrift without his steady guidance. The void was palpable, and I found myself questioning my next steps without his influence.

It was a difficult time of reflection and uncertainty. I had relied on his wisdom for so long, and without him, I wasn't sure if I could make the right decisions on my own. But in that void, I also realized something crucial: Bob had spent years shaping me into the leader I had become. While his physical presence was gone, his lessons remained deeply ingrained in me. He had equipped me with the tools I needed to navigate difficult decisions with trust, transparency, and kindness. I realized that, in many ways, he had prepared me for this very moment.

Though the impact of his loss was profound, it also pushed me to step into my own strength as a leader, carrying forward the legacy of his influence. Bob's guiding principles were still with me, shaping how I moved forward in both my career and in my life.

I had to make a choice: stay in my comfort zone or take a leap into the unknown. Not long after his passing, I received a recommendation from one of my ex-colleagues to pursue a position at another large organization—an opportunity that both excited and terrified me. It was a step up in my career, but I wasn't sure if I was ready to handle the challenges that came with such a move.

Taking that leap, buoyed by Bob's lessons and the trust of those I had worked with, was one of the toughest decisions I ever made.

I accepted the job, and unfortunately, I had a polar opposite experience.

Working for a company that was solely focused on the bottom line was a challenging and eye-opening experience. In an environment where profits and productivity were prioritized above all else, it became clear that the human element of the workplace often got lost in the numbers. Decisions were driven by spreadsheets rather than by the impact on employees or the suppliers that provided the company with the services we delivered to our customers. The constant pressure to meet targets created a culture of competition and burnout, where personal growth and well-being were secondary concerns.

It wasn't only about the long hours or the relentless push for higher margins—it was the feeling that people were seen as resources to be maximized, widgets, not as individuals with unique contributions to offer. Creativity was stifled, and collaboration often took a back seat to individual performance metrics. The focus on short-term gains overshadowed any long-term vision or commitment to fostering a positive, sustainable work environment. While I learned valuable lessons about efficiency and business strategy, the experience also deepened my understanding of the importance of balancing financial goals with compassion, integrity, and the well-being of the team.

chapter five

our selves

selfies, selfishness, self-esteem, and selflessness

You probably wouldn't worry about what people think of you if you could know how seldom they do.
—OLIN MILLER

Our society has become fixated on the "self" in unprecedented ways. This cultural shift has intensified a focus on personal image and identity, often to the point of selfishness. People are drawn to projecting curated versions of themselves, while the popularity of "self-love" has sometimes evolved into prioritizing oneself above all else. This chapter will explore the roots of this obsession, the effects it has on relationships and community, and how we might reclaim a sense of collective compassion in a culture increasingly focused on individualism.

We now live in a world so intertwined with technology that our focus is often absorbed by screens instead of the people around us. This constant engagement with technology has altered how we interact, diminishing the spontaneous exchanges and everyday kindnesses. The allure of the digital world has gradually taken precedence over the physical one, making it easier to overlook the faces, stories, and lives around us. It's a shift that calls for conscious effort to look up, engage, and remember the value of real human connection.

US adults spend an average of four to five hours a day on their phones.[6] Teens and tweens report similar numbers. In the book, *The Anxious Generation: How the Great Rewiring of Childhood is Causing an Epidemic of Mental Illness,* author and psychologist Jonathan Haidt discusses the toxicity of social media. According to the Centers for Disease Control and Prevention, 20 percent of kids aged twelve to seventeen have had at least one major depressive episode.[7] We are not OK as a society when it comes to this obsession and self-absorption.

The concepts of self-esteem and ego often seem blurred, yet they are fundamentally different. Self-esteem is rooted in a genuine appreciation and acceptance of who we are. It's about recognizing our own worth, feeling secure in our values, and treating ourselves with kindness, regardless of external validation. The ego, on the other hand, is often fueled by a need for external validation and can be more fragile, relying on comparisons or accolades to feel satisfied. While self-esteem is about inner confidence, ego often centers on the external desire to be seen as superior or important.

---

[6] Stacey Vanek Smith and Darian Woods, "How Much Phone Time Is Too Much Phone Time? Scientists Research Digital Addiction," *NPR,* August 13, 2021, https://www.npr.org/2021/08/13/1027317245/how-much-phone-time-is-too-much-phone-time-scientists-research-digital-addiction.

[7] Maura Kelly, "How to Calm the Anxious Generation," *Harvard Public Health,* accessed November 19, 2024, https://harvardpublichealth.org/mental-health/jonathan-haidt-on-countering-negative-effects-of-social-media/.

This confusion between self-esteem and ego has led many to believe that projecting self-importance is the same as possessing self-worth. True self-esteem is humble, and those who have it don't seek to elevate themselves at the expense of others. In contrast, a strong ego can create defensiveness, entitlement, or a need to prove oneself. By understanding this distinction, we can cultivate authentic self-esteem, focusing on growth and self-compassion rather than external validation. This shift allows for a more balanced, grounded approach to self-worth, emphasizing inner strength over outward status.

Unfortunately, during my adult life, there have been plenty of times when others have attempted to project their insecurities onto me. Whether through undermining, or dismissive behavior, these experiences were, of course, incredibly challenging. I suppose those people felt it was an easy way to gain power. And I have to admit that they made me question my abilities, value, and place in the world.

However, these moments have also taught me about the resilience and strength that come from maintaining a grounded sense of self. True self-esteem is built from within and can be remarkably resilient in the face of negativity. It's a continuous journey, but each experience strengthens our resolve to protect and nurture our own self-esteem, regardless of others' intentions.

When someone shows their true colors, believe them.

Perhaps we should look at such things as self-esteem and kindness as verbs rather than nouns or character traits. Self-esteem and kindness are not qualities we possess—they are revealed in the things we do through our actions and words. This shift in perspective empowers us to take responsibility for ourselves and transform this into a lifelong journey, rather than a fixed, unchanging state.

This requires an active, ongoing process that can eventually translate into the ways we speak to others (and to ourselves), the patience we offer, and the compassion we extend even in the smallest of interactions. By consciously incorporating such things into our everyday actions, they can eventually become habits. This simple daily commitment, with intent, can play an important role in making the world a better place, one thoughtful gesture at a time.

One thing I have learned throughout my journey of grief and trying to heal is that it is only through venturing outside ourselves that we can try to find grace and a modicum of peace. We need to become more aware of others and to prioritize character over appearance. I have found that the more I give, the more I heal.

Earth Angels have a unique ability to see the people around them with compassion and empathy, noticing the needs, struggles, and joys of others. They move through life with the intention of leaving each person and place a little better than they found them. This could be as simple as offering a smile to someone having a tough day, lending a helping hand, or listening with an open heart. Earth Angels are driven by the active, genuine desire to make the world kinder and more connected. Through small acts, they spread warmth and positivity, creating ripples of change that elevate everyone they encounter. Because of their presence, the world becomes a more compassionate, positive place.

> *Be nice to yourself. It's hard to be happy when someone's mean to you all the time.*
> —Christine Arylo

If only we could all accept ourselves for the individuals we are, without self-judgment or comparing ourselves to someone else—because this is always a lose–lose situation. As adults, we need to stop such negative behavior because, as I have already mentioned, kids are watching us. Yet, it's all too easy to fall back into old habits.

This was proven to me recently, when I was with my boys and I wanted to take a picture with them as a forever memory, and I wanted the picture to be perfect. After multiple takes, one of my sons looked at me and said, "Mom. You always tell us to be happy with who we are. If that's true, then why does it matter what you look like in the picture?" That is what I call a reality bitch slap. In the process of writing this chapter, I was guilty of the very thing I am writing about right now.

Again, it's a conscious, daily effort.

I'm guessing that many of you reading this book are nodding and can relate. In our selfie-obsessed world, a world of curated perfection, we seem to think we need to be perfect too. And we, of course, do not. A reminder for myself as well as every person reading this book.

Pay close attention to those around you at the next gathering when it's photo time. I'm sure you'll hear choruses of "I look horrible," "I'm too fat," "I hate this outfit," and so on. We're *incredibly* hard on ourselves. Or watch what happens after the photo is taken. Everyone will want to look at themself to decide if it's "good enough" to post online instead of feeling gratitude for a happy memory. Have you ever looked at a photo of a lost loved one and thought how horrible they looked? I doubt it. The fact of the matter is, those who love us just want that particular memory frozen in time.

In 2017, Cindy Crawford posted a throwback video of herself from the height of her career—with a caption, "Even I don't look like Cindy Crawford in the morning."[8]

---

[8] Hanna Fillingham, "Cindy Crawford Posts Amazing Throwback Footage Captioned: 'Even I Don't Wake Up Looking like Cindy Crawford,'" *Hello!*, July 24, 2017, https://www.hellomagazine.com/fashion/news/2017072457698/cindy-crawford-throwback-video-instagram/.

The next time you find yourself thinking negative thoughts—catch yourself. Simply recognizing when you are doing this is yet another action—a verb—and one that takes conscious effort. When we acknowledge these thoughts, we become aware of patterns that may be holding us back. This awareness allows us to question the validity of those thoughts, challenge any negative self-talk, and begin reframing it in a more compassionate, constructive way. This process of noticing, challenging, and reframing thoughts fosters inner confidence and keeps us moving forward with a stronger, more positive sense of self.

> *Be careful how you are talking to yourself because you are listening.*
> —Lisa M. Hayes

When I founded Shane's Imagine-Nation, I realized that helping kids develop self-awareness and self-esteem was vital. Those with self-awareness naturally possess self-esteem, and in turn, are kind to others. If I was going to combat negative behavior, these things would need to be essential building blocks. It's really important to me that the kids who participate in my programs leave feeling better about themselves and about life in general. I want them to know that they matter and that by simply practicing kindness toward others, they can start to recognize the impact they can have, and perhaps, most importantly, understand their own self-worth. Ultimately, I'd like them to be encouraged to leave their own positive forever footprint on the world.

CHAPTER FIVE

Selflessness

While there are many wonderful, kind people in the world, there are also countless wounded "mean" people out there. We cannot totally eradicate meanness; it's a societal illness. I like to think that the Earth Angel movement is analogous to an inoculation against a virus. Selfless acts combat selfishness. It directly challenges the ugly in the world. It won't fix it, but it will certainly combat it.

Here's the catch: Selflessness first calls us to eliminate the hypocrisies in our lives. As adults, we often fall into the "Do as I say, not as I do" mentality, even with the best of intentions. We tell our kids they're perfect just the way they are, encouraging them to love themselves and be confident, yet we are self-defeating in our own actions. We might criticize our appearance in front of the mirror or constantly downplay our accomplishments, sending mixed messages about self-worth. Kids pick up on this disconnect, noticing that while we tell them to embrace who they are, we struggle to do the same.

Our words ring pretty hollow.

In essence, while we strive to teach the right values, our actions sometimes reflect the opposite. It's a reminder to be more mindful of the behaviors we model, as children learn just as much, if not more, from what we do than what we say.

Selflessness, the act of putting others' needs before our own, requires us to step outside of our personal perspective and genuinely consider what someone else is going through. When we practice selflessness, we actively try to understand others' experiences, emotions, and challenges, allowing us to connect with their feelings on a deeper level. This connection is the essence of empathy—feeling *with* someone and understanding their emotions as if they were our own. It's about sharing their experience, not just observing it.

Having said that, the term empathy is very often confused with sympathy. While sympathy involves feeling *for* someone, it's often from a distance, with a sense of pity or compassion. Empathy involves a more active and personal engagement (another verb). It's about imagining what it's like to walk in someone else's shoes, experiencing their joy or pain alongside them, rather than simply acknowledging it from afar.

Through selflessness, we can cultivate the ability to see the world from others' perspectives, which naturally deepens our capacity for empathy. This connection allows us to respond with genuine care and understanding, rather than with detached sympathy.

A Teachable Moment

Several months ago, I was scrolling through my Facebook groups, and I came across a post written by a caregiver of a nonverbal adult with autism. He loved books, and every week, she would take him to the local library for children's story time, which brought him great joy. Her post was asking fellow group members their opinion on something that happened that day. Apparently, when the caregiver arrived at the regular time, she was told that she would no longer be able to attend story time because the gentleman was making people uncomfortable, even though he was nonverbal, gentle, and did nothing wrong. According to the library's staff, their policy stated the program was dedicated to children only.

It goes without saying that she received overwhelming support and outrage for the library's action. So much so that the story ended up on the evening news.

This could have (and should have) been a teachable moment to every child in the program about acceptance and diversity. Instead, the library sent a clear message that being different is not acceptable.

This man, always accompanied by his caregiver, was simply enjoying something that he loved and looked forward to every week.

Through its actions, the library missed the opportunity to lead by example. It not only failed the gentleman who so enjoyed weekly story time, but it failed every child who witnessed what happened.

Inspiring Selflessness

I love to collect stories of ordinary people—Earth Angels—making positive differences in others' lives through selflessness. I typically find them in media coverage, online, or people send me links about them because they know how much I love hearing about good people doing great things.

Sometimes a single unselfish act can transform a life.

I'll never forget the time I took the boys to a work event, where each child who attended was given several raffle tickets to win prizes. Each ticket was perforated, and each half had the same number. If someone wanted to win a prize, they would tear the ticket in half, put one half in the small bucket in front of the prize, and keep the other half to prove they had the winning number. There was excitement in the air as the kids clutched their tickets, imagining they might win. Shane, in particular, had his eye on a Play-Doh set. He wanted it so badly that he put all of his ticket halves in the bucket and carefully tucked the other halves in his pocket. Every now and again, I noticed him reaching into his pocket to make sure his tickets were still there, his face full of quiet anticipation.

As the time came to announce the winning numbers, Shane sat on the floor with the other kids, barely able to sit still. When it was time for the Play-Doh set, he was practically bouncing, clutching his tickets as each number was called. By the final number, he was on his knees, bursting with excitement. And when the final number was announced, he shot up, arms raised in victory, and started jumping up and down. He'd won the Play-Doh set he'd wanted so much.

As the event was ending and the kids gathered to get their coats, a woman approached me and asked if Shane was my son. I said yes. She then told me how her three-year-old daughter had been crying because she hadn't won the Play-Doh set. She was so young; she didn't yet understand about winning and losing. The mom told me that when Shane saw her daughter crying, without a second thought, he walked over to the girl, handed her the set, gave her a hug, and simply walked away. Shane didn't tell me what he had done. He did it out of the goodness of his heart, and it was never even mentioned until we were in the car on the way home, and I told him how proud I was that he was my son.

That experience exemplified Shane's selflessness and heart. He led by example, and that's why anyone who met him was better for it. His kindness didn't need attention; it was just who he was.

I must add here that it is not just Shane who embodies this spirit of selflessness—his brothers do as well. To me, that is a true gift that, no matter what else happens in my life, no one can ever take away.

One story that, frankly, still inspires me is featured in an episode of a documentary series on A&E called *Biography: WWE Legends* about the life of professional wrestler Booker T.[9]

---

9   *Biography: WWE Legends*, season 1, episode 4, "Booker T.," directed by George Roy, featuring Booker Huffman, Steve Austin, and Bonita Lott, aired May 9, 2021, on A&E, accessed December 19, 2024, https://www.imdb.com/title/tt14410236/.

CHAPTER FIVE

Booker T was only ten months old when his father died, leaving his mother to raise him and his siblings alone. When he was seven, the family moved to Houston, Texas, where his mother, a nurse, worked from eleven at night until seven in the morning in order to be there when the kids woke up and went to school and when they came home. Booker was extremely close to his mother and dreamed of one day buying her a house. As Booker said, his family was poor, but when you don't have something, you don't realize what you are missing.

Booker was only thirteen when his mother died.

The loss splintered the family, and in time, Booker succumbed to his surroundings. He spent eight months in jail and was ultimately sentenced to five years in prison.

When Booker was seventeen, still a child himself, he had a son. Unfortunately, the boy's mother was addicted to drugs, so the child was sent into foster care. In prison, Booker was able to take a step back and reflect on what he wanted his life—and his son's—to be. He knew he had a choice. So, he got his GED and worked in the laundry room. He fully committed himself to becoming a better person. I believe that had it not been for the love and devotion of his mother, Booker would have become merely a statistic.

After nineteen months, Booker was released on parole. On his way out, one of the guards looked at him and said, "I'll see you when you get back." Instead of supporting Booker and believing in him, that guard exemplified the opposite of an Earth Angel. Yet, Booker decided that his life would forever be what he was going to make of it, and he would never listen to the noise. Booker's first priority was to get his son back, but he knew, given the circumstances, this would not be an easy task.

Upon his release from prison, Booker asked his brother Lash for help finding a job. He knew he had a long road ahead, but his eyes were set on the goal of getting his son back. Lash eventually helped Booker land a job as—of all things for a person fresh out of prison—a security guard. Booker lived with his brother for approximately one year in order to prove to the "system" that he had learned from his mistakes, was a good citizen, and would be a great father to his now five-year-old son.

When the security company's manager learned of Booker's past incarceration, Booker was relieved of his position. However, after getting to know Booker's character and work ethic, the manager hired him to manage various operations for his own storage unit facility. The manager believed in Booker, recognized what he was capable of, and—as Earth Angels do—enabled him to look to the future instead of dwelling on and being defined by the past. Booker excelled.

One day, Booker's brother Lash learned of a wrestling school, and the brothers wanted nothing more than to attend. As kids, they had loved watching professional wrestling together and had even transformed an old mattress into a wrestling ring. Unfortunately, the tuition for the school was $4,000, far outside of Booker's budget. The same manager who had given Booker a second chance to succeed believed in him so much that he paid the tuition for him to attend the school. This selfless act ultimately changed many lives—for the better—forever. The ripple effect again.

As Booker advanced in his wrestling career, other mentors and supporters continued to invest in him, helping him develop and hone his skill, talent, and confidence. This belief from others helped Booker recognize his potential and pushed him to work harder, stay disciplined, and make the most of every opportunity. Despite facing barriers and life obstacles, Booker's resilience, combined with the encouragement he received, allowed him to rise through the ranks of the wrestling world, becoming a six-time world champion, and on April 6, 2013, Booker was inducted into the WWE Hall of Fame by his brother Lash.

Booker's journey demonstrates how selflessness, and the belief and support of others, can be the catalyst for personal transformation. Other people's faith in him helped Booker see beyond his circumstances and envision a future where he could achieve greatness, proving that with the right support, people can rise above even the most challenging circumstances.

This is exactly what this book is about—because ordinary actions can (and often do) leave an extraordinary impact. This is what Earth Angels do.

There is no shortage of stories like this. Acts of selflessness are happening at this very moment. To be selfless . . . we must listen. Act. Inspire.

The choice is yours to make.

Please Join Me

I believe that many of the world's major problems are rooted in selfishness and ego, driving behaviors that prioritize individual desires over the collective good. Selfishness creates a mentality where people focus solely on their own needs, ambitions, and conveniences, often at the expense of others. It fuels greed, corruption, and the exploitation of resources, leading to inequality, suffering, and the intentional harming of others. When ego takes the lead, this fosters a desire for power, dominance, and control, creating division and conflict between people, groups, and nations.

We find ourselves trapped in battles over status, pride, and personal gain. This fixation on self can blind us to the struggles of others and diminish our capacity for empathy and collaboration. I believe that true progress, healing, and peace can only be achieved when we actively shift our focus away from self-centeredness, begin to value compassion and understanding, and gain a sense of shared responsibility for the world we all inhabit.

In the end, "self" is an active, evolving concept—a balance of selfishness and selflessness that requires conscious action. Being selfish isn't inherently negative; it's setting boundaries, meeting your needs, and prioritizing well-being. Selflessness, meanwhile, is about extending care and kindness to others, nurturing relationships, and creating a positive impact. These aren't fixed traits; they're verbs—actions that require daily effort and intention. To live fully, we must do both: We must honor our own needs while giving to others. Each choice we make shapes our "self," reflecting that who we are is not a static identity but a continuous, active pursuit of balance.

It has been extremely humbling to learn about the ways Shane has influenced so many others. In fact, to this day, I continue to receive notes and messages from people about Shane as well as stories of strange coincidences that are so extraordinary that they could not be mere coincidences at all.

When Shane got on the school bus on April 25, 2018, I know he didn't want to die. I was with him as he stepped onto the bus. He was my typical happy, positive Shane. He didn't have to die. He should not have died. And, ultimately, this is one part of his story to tell: We all must take a step back and recognize the impact we have on others.

Simple Earth Angel actions can change someone's life. Then, a community. Then, in turn, these little things together can change the world.

Life happens to or for you. Don't talk about "someday." Make today the day.

chapter six

cultivating kindness online

technology and earth angels

Beauty is only skin deep, but ugly goes clean to the bone.
—DOROTHY PARKER

The scale of online harmful behavior is vast, as technology enables bullies to reach their targets at any time, any place, eroding the boundary between personal and digital spaces. In this chapter, we'll explore the far-reaching consequences of online bullying and discuss what we can do to protect ourselves and others in an increasingly connected, yet vulnerable, world.

It seems to me that online bullying is a manifestation of a larger, systemic issue within our society—one that is deeply rooted in the way we communicate, perceive power, and treat one another. It thrives in a culture that often highlights aggression, encourages competition over empathy, and places a high value on appearances and social status.

In a world where social media and digital interactions are an integral part of daily life, these underlying societal dynamics are amplified online, allowing harmful behaviors to spread much more easily and with far greater impact.

Part of the systemic nature of online bullying is that the digital world can create a sense of anonymity and distance, making it easier for individuals to act without facing immediate consequences. This lack of accountability can encourage behaviors that would likely be restrained in face-to-face interactions. At the same time, our society often struggles to equip young people with the tools they need to navigate online spaces with kindness and empathy. Schools, parents, and communities may not always have the resources or strategies to address these issues effectively, leaving many young people vulnerable to the psychological harm that online bullying can inflict.

Furthermore, online platforms themselves can inadvertently foster toxic environments, with algorithms that prioritize sensational, often inflammatory, content because it generates more engagement. This creates a cycle where negative interactions gain more visibility and traction, perpetuating a culture where bullying and harassment can feel normalized.

Addressing online bullying requires a shift in how we, as a society, value empathy, respect, and kindness, both online and offline. It involves educating people about the impact of their words, holding platforms accountable for creating safer digital spaces, and encouraging a culture that values genuine connection over aggression and harmful behavior. Ultimately, online bullying is not just an individual issue; it reflects deeper societal problems that require collective action to change.

CHAPTER SIX

Social Media: A World of Curated Perfection

> *The trick of the internet, I had learned, was not being unapologetically yourself or completely unfiltered; it was mastering the trick of appearing that way. It was spiking your posts with just the right amount of real . . . which meant, of course, that you were never being real at all.*
> —Jennifer Weiner, Big Summer

Imagine scrolling through social media, where every image is carefully selected, every angle perfected, every caption polished. As you watch, it's easy to feel inadequate, to wonder why your life doesn't match the curated images others put on display.

While social media platforms offer many benefits, such as connecting with friends and family, humorous memes, and special interest groups, they can also pose serious problems. Every time we scroll through any social media platform, we are bombarded with perfectly posed selfies and curated selves. These deceptive portrayals often come at a cost, particularly to kids, who can develop unrealistic standards at a time when they are still trying to figure out who they are. Unfortunately, many kids are turning to social media looking for role models, whose validation is seen in their number of followers, likes, comments, etc. For many, social media has become a metric of measurement for self-worth.

This focus on perfectionism is dangerous because it inevitably leads to failure. The pressure to live up to unrealistic standards can result in low self-esteem, diminished self-worth, and an increase in self-criticism. Influencers who feel compelled to present an idealized version of themselves—a facade of happiness and success—can foster a culture of comparison and pressure to conform. When you think about it, very few people post their flaws, yet when we see unedited images, we find them refreshing.

All is not lost, though. More and more often, we are seeing influencers who are normalizing imperfections and emphasizing self-acceptance. Presenting a humanized version of themselves and prioritizing authenticity and relatability can foster empathy and deeper connections. Understanding the implications curated perfection can have on mental health and self-esteem is a great first step to normalizing values and character instead of external validation.

The Dark Side of Online Anonymity

The percentage of people who have experienced cyberbullying at some point in their lifetime is growing exponentially. In fact, 41 percent of US adult internet users since 2021 have reported some form of online abuse or harassment.[10] The fact of the matter is, social media is part of our everyday lives. Nothing is going to change until we each change what we are doing.

Almost every second in the hours, days, weeks, and yes, even years, after Shane's death, I have wandered in a thick fog of grief that just won't go away. I work extremely hard to stay ahead of it; keeping busy, sharing Shane's story, and promoting kindness through Shane's Imagine-Nation has worked thus far. This is not to say that I don't have moments when I shut down and isolate myself. I wish I could

---

10   Stacy Jo Dixon, "U.S. Internet Users Who Have Experienced Cyber Bullying 2021," *Statista*, accessed November 19, 2024, https://www.statista.com/statistics/333942/us-internet-online-harassment-severity/.

say that the dark days are diminishing as time goes on, but they aren't. Keeping busy and having a purpose is something that keeps me going because there is so much work to be done. The truth is, if I don't keep busy, I feel like I'd lose my mind. As a mom, it was my job to protect my child. I will always feel that I somehow failed Shane. My life will forever be marked as my life with Shane, and my life after Shane. I will never allow Shane's death to be in vain.

I used to post a lot on social media, particularly uplifting messages and affirmations, because sometimes we just need to know that we aren't alone, and that we are all perfectly imperfect. I make a point to always be authentic, which, of course, means being vulnerable. Shortly after losing Shane, an online troll felt the need to respond to one of my posts. The post has long since been deleted, but the gist of the vile message was that if I was a good mother, my child would not have taken his own life and he would still be alive.

Replies to my posts had always been positive, so this particular comment made my stomach drop and my body become ice cold. I instantly broke down and experienced a very scary panic attack. This person, a total stranger, had (and has) no idea of the guilt I feel every day and how I'll be haunted for the rest of my life, trying to figure out what I missed and what I could have done to save my son's life. There was no way I was going to respond to this person (although it was tough to hold back). Over and over, I had to remind myself that if I unleashed and engaged, it would make me a hypocrite. Yet, I kept asking myself why or how anyone would feel so inclined to intentionally hurt me like this? The comment was hurtful and harmful, and something I'll never forget.

Thankfully, a good friend of mine did respond, and in a very powerful and profound way. She made it clear to anyone reading the post how inappropriate and hideous the comment was. She told the troll that if he had witnessed me lying silently in a fetal position next to Shane, who was on life support—never leaving his side, playing his favorite Broadway music next to his ear in the hopes that it would trigger something and he would regain brain function—he would know how heart-wrenchingly painful it was. He would understand what it was like to know my son would die as soon as organ recipients were found. She said she would never wish that experience on anyone.

As I lay next to Shane, all I could think was that—somewhere in the world—people would live, while Shane would give his last selfless act of kindness.

My friend was righteously indignant—furious—over someone who did not know me deciding they could pass judgment. It's impossible for me to *fathom* what would possess a human being to say the most hurtful thing possible to a parent who just lost their child to suicide. I'm also quite confident this person would have never said it to my face.

A few months after losing Shane, I wrote the following journal entry, because the minute we lost him, I knew that somewhere—I would never know where or who—there were several people walking the earth because of Shane's selfless gift to them. That Shane had selflessly saved their lives.

I wanted them to know what a gift of love they had received:

AN OPEN LETTER TO THE RECIPIENTS OF SHANE'S ORGANS

Exactly one year ago today, almost to the very moment I am typing this, was a day just like any other. I woke up at six a.m., got my boys up to get ready for school, got them onto the bus, and I went off to work. There was nothing unusual about anything. The night prior, the same thing. I always made sure to try to keep weekday evenings during the school year as routine as possible. I'd come home from work, kiss the boys hello and ask them how their days were, go upstairs to change, come downstairs, and pour myself a glass of wine and relax for about fifteen minutes before getting up to make dinner. During this time, the boys would get showered and finish their homework so that we could all eat together, talk about things, and spend quality time together. After dinner, we would cuddle on the couch and watch TV before they would be told it's bedtime. So, off they go, always complaining that it is too early for bedtime and how none of their friends must go to bed that early, etc. What they didn't realize is that I knew by the time they got upstairs, brushed their teeth, and finally got settled in, it would be hours later anyway. Three boys tend not to go straight to sleep, as they talk, talk, talk, so the routine bedtime was based off the assumption, and confirmation, that no one would be asleep before 9:30/10:00 p.m. anyway. And the fact of the matter is that the bus arrived at 6:45 a.m., and I knew full well by experience that getting three sleepy, grouchy little fellows off to school was no easy task. Nothing was different. Yet—everything was completely different. Had I known that the moment I kissed him goodbye and got him on the bus would be the last time I would ever see my baby alive again, I would have never let him go. Every single day is painful for me. Every day something new will remind me that Shane is not here with me.

My grief and despair are equally as bad now as they were that day—one year ago. April 25, 2018—what seemed to be a perfectly normal day immediately and unexpectedly turned into the worst day of my life.

Donating Shane's organs wasn't even my idea. The truth is, I was in deep shock, denial, and heavily medicated. It was Shane's brothers—grieving kids themselves—boys who had lost their childhoods forever that day—who were able to think of others—you—throughout the worst time of their own lives.

I say this because I want you to get a perspective, an idea of the goodness and beauty that live within my children. Their selfless natures are only one teeny fraction of the blessed qualities that each of them possesses, and this is something that you should know.

I have written this letter because I need you to know who Shane was, and how exquisite of a human being he was, and how his spirit is, and will continue to inspire many. You are now an inherent part of my soul, my baby, my love, my "monkey bear" (this was my nickname for Shane because when he was a baby, he would climb up my body like a little monkey climbing a tree and wrap his arms and legs around me like a koala bear—monkey bear). You have been given a gift far greater than I believe you will ever know.

I must admit something. Because I am writing this letter from a place of truth. While, as a fellow human being, I am deeply happy that you have a future that perhaps you did not have one year ago today, the instinctual and maternal piece of me—the mommy—feels resentment I never knew I'd have. I am an honest, good person—but I am also a mom who lost her son. A person who will most certainly never feel true happiness again, because there will always be something missing.

I now have only two kids to count, not three. My instincts still (and likely always will) prompt me to get three of everything: three Easter baskets, three donuts from Dunkin' Donuts, three hoodies when I can get away to surprise them with a present from my travels, three kids to feed, cuddle, and love. Three to two becomes an infinite void that will never be filled.

CHAPTER SIX

Right now, there is someone on this earth with Shane's beautiful heart. A heart that was certainly crafted from fine gold. An open, caring, loving heart. A heart that only felt the good in this world, that turned a negative into a positive no matter what (even when Santa said he wouldn't bring anything but coal[11], Shane was happy that Mommy could have a warm house and maybe one day a big diamond from said coal). A heart filled with empathy I have yet to find in another human being. A heart so precious that Shane would give away his prized possessions because he just loved to make others happy and always spoke about the looks on their faces when he did. So, whoever you are—you need to know how truly special that heart is that is now beating with life inside of you, each beat feeding you with the life that I so long to still have with me.

Please take great care of that heart and continue to spread the love that Shane so selflessly always did. And each time you feel its rhythm—I ask that you try to think of Shane, one of the most amazing human beings there ever was—as a final gift from him—to you.

I wonder if you are reading this because you are now able to see through Shane's eyes: If you can see the sheer beauty in the world, in the littlest things, as Shane always did. If you can read this, you need to know that Shane saw the world differently than most people. Shane found goodness and beauty in everything and everyone. Not only did Shane compliment people, even strangers (we used to call it the "Miss Crabtree moment"—if you know the Little Rascals, you know what I mean). Shane was known for finding the shape of a heart everywhere we went, no matter where or when— there was

---

11   One early morning in mid-December when the boys were young, I was driving them to school, and they kept arguing in the back seat. I repeatedly told them to stop, but, of course, they didn't. So I pulled over, turned around, and said, "If you don't stop fighting, Santa won't leave any presents; he will just leave coal."

always a heart to be found: in raindrops, clouds, strawberries, stones, shadows, anything—I can go on and on . . . That says a lot about him, I think.

I also called Shane my "rainbow hunter" because after a storm, Shane seemed to always be the first to find the rainbow in the sky. Trust me, there was a competition. So, if you are one of the people who can see through Shane's eyes, the next time you notice a heart or a rainbow—or simply see beauty in something, no matter how insignificant it may seem—please know that Shane was beautiful too, inside and outside. And, oh, his eyes. His beautiful almond-shaped, brown eyes—perfect eyes—I always asked him where he thought he got them from because they were unlike any in the family. Those perfect eyes perfectly symbolize the person Shane was, just beauty and perfection, unlike any other.

I've heard that someone received Shane's lungs—the lungs that breathed life into my baby's body. The lungs that filled with the air of joy or anticipation on Christmas morning, before he blew out his birthday candles on his cake, waiting for a Broadway show to start, the night I won a cooking competition for our family's sauerbraten recipe: That deep inhalation of breath, of life, air that was slowly released or quickly exhaled—depending on the situation.

I cannot tell you how many times Shane and I were together walking, usually hand in hand (he was not ashamed of me, thankfully!)—making memories and just talking about things. I am so grateful that I have never taken a moment for granted. Every breath Shane took was one taken with gratitude by me. I pray that you feel that gratitude as well, because the breaths we each take on this earth have a finite number—while Shane's has ended—yours has begun, and each breath you take please try to remember how pure and awesome they had been being protected by my Shane.

CHAPTER SIX

Each year on Halloween (our favorite, and it was a huge deal in my house—we even made our house and barn into walkthrough haunted houses), Shane would have a vision in mind as to what he wanted to be. But it was never (not once) the typical costume selected by someone his age. For example: I took him to Alcatraz when he was just old enough to know what Halloween is (and to show him what can happen to "bad people"), and in the two weeks until Halloween, Shane decided he wanted to be "the Birdman of Alcatraz." Since then, his costumes became even more specific and the last two years of his life, his specific vision required that he sit in a chair for over two hours with me painting a special glue to his face used for such purposes. He sat there so patiently, and I had no idea what I was doing, other than the occasional break to watch a YouTube instructional video. He didn't complain, but all I kept thinking was the fumes he could be breathing into those precious lungs, so all the windows were open, and I made him take breaks to ensure he was OK. I was so careful to make sure he didn't inhale the fumes—so that I could protect the lungs that now protect you. But, when he was able to see the final result, the massive inhalation of surprise and giddiness, his face beaming with excitement and pride knowing that I was able to transform him into what he had envisioned in his own mind.

The lungs that now fill with air, used to be filled with gratitude, pride, and joy. I can tell you more often than anyone I have ever met. The lungs that gave my baby boy life, the second he was born and that anticipated newborn baby cry—now belong to you. So, please take the time to smell the flowers. This is something Shane and I did all the time. Perhaps he knew his time was short, perhaps he knew he had a reason. I will never know, but I ask that you understand this. Please take the time to appreciate the things that most people take for granted. For, this is what life is about.

I want you to know that I have dedicated my life to ensuring that what happened to Shane doesn't happen to another child.

Hate kills. Hate killed Shane. The one with the golden heart, eyes that see only beauty, and lungs that beamed with the joy of being alive.

I wish I could have prevented his heart from being broken because of the cruelty of kids who will likely never know the love everyone has for Shane.

I wish I could have wiped the tears that must have streamed out of those beautiful old-soul eyes that fell down his beautiful face.

I wish I could tell him how much I love him, cuddle with him, hold his warm hand, and feel him just breathing precious air. I just want him home safe, with me.

Please know that while I am extremely happy for you, and we may never even meet, all I ask is that you please, please take good care of yourself. Because if you are alive, a part of Shane is alive too, and this brings me comfort.

Very sincerely yours,
Sandy—Shane's Proud Mom

I hope that the online troll who made that wounding comment is reading this book right now.

Sadly, online bullying is more common than you may think. In fact,

- about 53 percent of teenagers say they have been subjected to online harassment or bullying;[12]

- students are almost twice as likely to attempt suicide if they have been cyberbullied;[13]

- 37 percent of bullying victims develop social anxiety;[14]

- 14.5 percent of children between the ages of nine and twelve have been cyberbullied;[15] and

- among adults, the figures are just as discouraging, with roughly 40 percent having experienced online harassment.[16]

In truth, I don't know if Shane was abused online. The police report, which is about four inches thick, is still sealed in the FedEx envelope it was in when I received it. It would be absolutely impossible for me to read in detail what happened to my son. Some may disagree, wondering how I could not want to know. But I do know this: I wouldn't be able to recover from it. I don't want to know who the kids were who bullied Shane, because I've made a conscious decision to help kids, not hate them.

I did, however, write a hypothetical letter to them (which I knew I would never send). I'm including it in this book because it's important

---

12   Katherine Schaeffer, "9 Facts About Bullying in the U.S.," *Pew Research Center*, November 17, 2023, https://www.pewresearch.org/short-reads/2023/11/17/9-facts-about-bullying-in-the-us/.

13   Ivana Vojinovic, "Heart-Breaking Cyberbullying Statistics," *DataProt*, updated February 6, 2024, https://dataprot.net/statistics/cyberbullying-statistics/.

14   Ibid.

15   Ibid.

16   Emily A. Vogels, "The State of Online Harassment," *Pew Research Center*, January 13, 2021, https://www.pewresearch.org/internet/2021/01/13/the-state-of-online-harassment/#:~:text=A%20Pew%20Research%20Center%20survey%20of%20U.S.%20adults,of%20the%20six%20key%20ways%20that%20were%20measured.

for anyone reading this to never forget that behind every instance of pain is a human story. The purpose of this book is to discourage abusive behaviors and encourage the Earth Angels around us.

There is no doubt in my mind that, had those kids known what a beautiful human being Shane was, they would surely never have hurt him.

AN OPEN LETTER TO THE KID(S) WHO BULLIED MY SON SHANE:

I know you are too young to grasp the impact that your words and actions had on my son, yet I still hold you responsible. You know what is right from what is wrong, yet there is so much you didn't know.

When you called him "gay," what you didn't know is that he and I had a bond unlike any other. As a result, he tended to feel more comfortable with and trust women. He knew we were nurturing.

He understood unconditional love because I would never hurt him. You and your posse of friends saw my son with a gaggle of girls . . . Perhaps you now have a better understanding of why he decided to surround himself with people he trusted. Your actions must have only reinforced to him that some people can't be trusted or respected.

When you made fun of him for loving music and theater, what you didn't see was the light in my son's eyes when he saw a play and the complete appreciation and passion that he had for it. He only wanted to share his passion with others.

What you didn't know is that he saved his birthday money to buy a ticket for one of his friends who had never seen a play. This selfless act is only a tiny example of the innate goodness that existed within that tiny body. Because of this passion and enthusiasm, you taunted him, ridiculed him, and acted so cruelly. I very much doubt you have ever found something to become that passionate about. That is sad.

When you laughed at him, what you didn't know is how hard he always tried to fit in and be liked. That all he wanted was to be accepted for the amazing human being he was. He looked up to kids like you to determine his self-worth regardless of how many times I had told him how amazing he is and how others' perceptions of him are meaningless.

When you called him "retarded," what you didn't know is that he was diagnosed with ADD when he was in kindergarten, which clearly only further outcasted him from people like you. What you didn't know is how hard I fought to find a solution to why my son could not sit still or control his behavior.

What you didn't know is how extraordinarily intelligent my son was. How his wit made me laugh every single day and how he knew more about most things than I do. How inherently proud I was of him for always turning a negative into a positive, which you will learn many people can't do.

When you made fun of his clothes and the way he dressed, what you didn't know is that I am a single mother struggling to make ends meet. And while your clothes may come from the mall, my sons' came from thrift stores and hand-me-downs. But . . . he appreciated all that he had because he knew how hard I worked for them.

When you made fun of the shirts that he proudly wore from the money he had saved on his own of the various Broadway shows he had seen, what you didn't know is that underneath that shirt was a heart of gold. Which thanks to you is gone forever.

What you didn't know is that he would never let you see him cry. He was smart enough to understand it would only add fuel to the fire.

What you didn't know is that the words you have spoken are like weapons. But unlike a cut, your words scarred him deep within his soul. Perhaps with time they would have faded. But this I will never know.

What you didn't know is that I will forever be haunted by the humiliation and pain you caused my son.

However, it will never compare to the humiliation and pain he must have felt. If I am being honest, I am not ready to know exactly how long he suffered, because it will put me down a hole I don't want to go down. I would most likely never come out of it either.

You didn't know your words and actions had seeped into his brain and made him believe that what you said to him was true. He eventually shut down and gave up.

Perhaps, with time, I will forgive you. Perhaps not.

Perhaps my son could have forgotten the things you have said and done to him. Perhaps not. I will never know.

I fear that my son would have carried these scars with him for the rest of his life. For, someday in the future, something would have triggered a memory of what you have done: a song, a smell, a voice . . . and would have brought him right back to that moment where he was a vulnerable little boy who only wanted to fit in and be liked.

I will never again have the opportunity to hold him, kiss him, and tell him that everything is going to be OK, because it won't be. What you don't know is that Shane's older brothers have had their childhoods stolen from them too. They will never be the same again because their brother is gone forever.

CHAPTER SIX

What you don't know is that I cry myself to sleep every night. That I hide my pain from my boys because they need to know that I am OK, so that they can be OK.

What most don't know is that this is the hardest thing I have ever had to do in my life. That this is not about being strong or courageous—it is surviving.

What you don't know is the pain I feel when I walk past Shane's empty room, still exactly the way he left it. His bed is still unmade, and his water bottle is still on his nightstand.

Shane's bedroom, exactly how he left it on April 25, 2018.

I will not feel sorry for you. The fact that my son was a lesson for you to learn is something that I am not willing to forgive.

I cannot imagine how unhappy you must be with yourself. Kind people are kind. Happy people spread kindness. The fact that you could say such cruel things only exemplifies how you must feel about yourself. Oftentimes, the most important lessons are learned the hard way.

You may have apologized for what you have done, but you reap what you sow. I promise you that no matter what happens in your life—you will never know the love that I will always have for my sons.

Sincerely,
Sandy (Shane's Proud Mom)

What Can We Do?

> I speak to everyone in the same way, whether he is the garbage man or the president of the university.
> —Albert Einstein

The behavior of online trolls reveals an ugly side of human nature—one that thrives on negativity, cruelty, and the dehumanization of others. Hidden behind screens and often cloaked in anonymity, trolls use the distance of the digital world to spread insults, provoke anger, and sow discord without facing the direct consequences of their actions. This anonymity strips away the basic social accountability that typically governs face-to-face interactions, allowing some people to act in ways they might never dare to in person. The result is behavior that is often shockingly hostile, targeting others' vulnerabilities and seeking to intentionally inflict emotional pain.

CHAPTER SIX

Trolls often prey on those who are already marginalized or vulnerable, using words and images to tear others down in ways that are intensely personal and hurtful. They exploit differences, such as race, gender, sexuality, or beliefs, turning them into weapons to ridicule, shame, and belittle. This behavior is not only damaging to individuals but also to the broader online communities, fostering a toxic environment where people may feel unsafe or discouraged from sharing their own thoughts and experiences.

What makes trolling especially insidious is that it thrives on eliciting reactions, no matter how harmful. Trolls often take pleasure in the chaos they create, taking advantage of the internet's speed and reach to amplify their harmful messages. They exploit moments of vulnerability, such as grief or loss, with shocking insensitivity, demeaning those who are already hurting. This reflects a deeper problem in how we perceive empathy and accountability online, where some feel empowered to act without compassion.

> *Knowing what's right doesn't mean much unless you do what's right.*
> —Theodore "Teddy" Roosevelt

Combating this ugliness means calling out harmful behavior, fostering online spaces that prioritize respect, and challenging the systems that allow trolls to hide behind their screens without facing the consequences of their cruelty.

We tend to get so caught up in our own lives that it's really easy to forget that, at this moment, there are millions of people suffering in silence. As I wrote earlier in the book, as we get older, the term bullying morphs into something else entirely. Yet, when we recognize it, we don't call it out. We have to get serious about creating a space without such rampant intentional malice. It's been drilled into our heads everywhere we go—if you "see something, say something." I encourage the same vigilance toward online bullying and toxic behavior, for they are their own breed of weapon.

If the ugliness of online trolls is a disease, then *action*—by empathy, kindness, and vulnerability—is the cure. It's time to lead by example because you can bet that the next generation—tomorrow's leaders—is watching us. We can't change others; we can only change ourselves.

> *The reason we struggle with insecurity is because we compare our behind-the-scenes with everyone else's highlight reel.*
> —Steven Furtick

Online toxicity isn't just isolated to trolls and hurtful comments. It also includes the curated perfection so many people attempt to portray. This isn't real life, and it's certainly not realistic. Understanding the implications that this can have on mental health and self-esteem is vital because so many people are, as the quote above makes clear, comparing themselves to someone else's highlight reel.

Comparing your reality to someone else's carefully constructed illusion can have serious consequences on self-worth, mental health, and overall happiness. Comparing ourselves to others, especially to their online personas, is like judging a book by its cover—a cover that has been meticulously crafted to project an ideal. But just like the cover of a book can't convey the complexity within its pages, someone's social media posts can't capture the full spectrum of their lives. You're not seeing their struggles, insecurities, or failures. And yet, seeing their "perfect" life can make you feel that something is wrong with yours.

Why Comparison Can Be So Harmful

> *Wanting to be someone else is a waste of the person you are.*
> *—Marilyn Monroe*

The toxicity of online curated perfection lies in its ability to distort reality, setting unattainable standards that many people strive to emulate—often to their own detriment. Social media platforms have become showcases for idealized versions of life, where carefully selected photos, edited images, and filtered moments create a constant stream of perfection. These images can make it seem as though everyone else is living a flawless, joy-filled life, where struggles and imperfections do not exist. This relentless display of curated content can lead to feelings of inadequacy, envy, and anxiety as people compare their authentically real, messy lives to unattainable ideals.

This culture of perfection also encourages people to hide their vulnerabilities, fears, and challenges, portraying only their most polished, curated selves. It promotes the idea that success and happiness must always look a certain way, pushing aside the reality that life's true richness comes from its complexities, imperfections, the messy process of growth, and lessons learned the hard way. The pressure to appear perfect online can create a sense of isolation, as people feel unable to share their authentic selves or reach out for support when they are struggling. It turns platforms that could foster genuine connection into spaces where validation is sought through likes and follows rather than through meaningful interactions.

Moreover, this culture contributes to a cycle of inauthenticity, where the pressure to maintain a perfect image is passed on from one person to another. It can negatively impact mental health, leading to issues such as low self-esteem, body image concerns, and a constant fear of not measuring up. The curated perfection of social media can make people forget that life is meant to be imperfect, full of ups and downs, and that everyone faces challenges, no matter how flawless their online presence might appear.

Ultimately, the toxicity of curated perfection is that it denies the value of being real and human. It overlooks the beauty in vulnerability and the strength in authenticity. Challenging this culture means embracing and celebrating our true selves—our struggles, our flaws, and all the things that make us uniquely human. It means creating online spaces where people feel safe to be real, and where connection is built on truth rather than illusion.

Comparison, especially with others' best moments, often leads to a distorted self-image. Research has shown that people who frequently engage in social comparison tend to experience higher levels of depression, anxiety, and envy. Psychologists call this "social comparison theory," which suggests that comparing ourselves to others can trigger feelings of inferiority and low self-esteem. This constant comparison traps us in a cycle of wanting more—more success, more happiness, more validation. But instead of achieving these goals, we're often left feeling like we're falling short. Academic, author, and TED speaker Brené Brown explains that this leads to a sense of "scarcity" or the belief that "I'm not enough," which perpetuates feelings of inadequacy. This gap between perception and reality can lead to self-criticism and unrealistic expectations.

CHAPTER SIX

Reframing the Narrative

> *Consider the fact that maybe . . . just maybe . . . beauty and worth aren't found in a makeup bottle, or a salon-fresh hairstyle, or a fabulous outfit. Maybe our sparkle comes from somewhere deeper inside, somewhere so pure and authentic and REAL, it doesn't need gloss or polish or glitter to shine.*
> —Mandy Hale

The antidote to comparison is shifting the focus inward. Instead of measuring yourself against someone else's life, consider what brings you meaning and fulfillment. Reflect on your achievements, even (or especially) the small ones, and appreciate your own journey. When we can prioritize growth over perfection, we can start to see life for what it is—a unique, personal journey that can't be captured in a single snapshot, selfie, or false persona.

Social media can inspire, but it's essential to remember that real life is far messier and much more complex. By setting aside comparisons and embracing what makes us unique, we can cultivate confidence and a deeper sense of contentment that's resilient in the face of adversity and, of course, others' curated highlights.

Our mindsets must shift. We have to stop and ask ourselves tough questions about how we interact with and use social media. And, as has been shown in multiple studies, we are spending more and more time online. In the US, we average two hours twenty-seven minutes every day on social media.[17] This is dangerous—and potentially harmful to our emotional and social well-being. When was the last time you stepped outside of your comfort zone and meaningfully interacted with those around you? When was the last time you sat down with your family and enjoyed a meal without someone looking at their phone?

A few years ago, I took my boys to see the house that I grew up in on Dobbs Ferry Road in New York. Everyone was hungry, so I decided to stop at an Italian restaurant I had driven by countless times but had never experienced. The moment we were seated, the waiter placed a basket at the table and instructed each of us to place our smart phones in the basket. The house rule was that no one was allowed to use their phone in the restaurant. They wanted their diners to connect with each other. It was absolutely brilliant, and the boys talk about that place to this day.

I encourage you, if you are a parent, to talk to your kids about this as well because we know the online universe can be full of misleading, dangerous, and cruel content.

Consider the following questions when analyzing your own or your children's online activity:

1. **What is my primary purpose for using social media?**
2. **How much time am I spending online daily?**
3. **How do I feel after spending time online?**
4. **Am I engaging in meaningful and positive interactions?**
5. **Do I often compare myself to others online?**
6. **Am I consuming reliable and diverse sources of information?**

---

[17] Lyndon Seitz, "Average Daily Time Spent on Social Media (Latest 2024 Data)," *BroadbandSearch*, last modified April 18, 2024, https://www.broadbandsearch.net/blog/average-daily-time-on-social-media.

7. How do I handle disagreements or negative comments?

8. Is my online behavior consistent with my offline values and principles?

9. Am I mindful of my digital footprint?

When posting online, ask yourself the following:

- T: Is it true?
- H: Is it helpful?
- I: Is it inspiring?
- N: Is it necessary?
- K: Is it kind?

10. Do I take regular breaks and set boundaries for my online activity?

By regularly asking yourself these questions, you can become more mindful of your online habits and ensure that your internet use contributes positively.

chapter seven

finding your superpower

what mark will you leave on the world?

Find out who you are and do it on purpose.
—DOLLY PARTON

Earth Angels are those who use their unique qualities—their superpowers—to make a positive impact on the world around them. While they may not have literal wings or capes, their actions and intentions can foster healing, hope, and kindness in profound ways.

My son Shane had superpowers. His kindness was woven into everything he did, and his story serves as the heart of this book. Throughout his life, Shane found beauty in the smallest details, finding hearts in everything—whether a stone on the sidewalk, a quirky shape in his bowl of cereal, or a fleeting raindrop on the window, he would point out these tiny, heart-shaped wonders, each one making him smile like he'd discovered a treasure. Shane was also always the first to spot a rainbow. As I wrote in the letter to the recipients of

Shane's organs, one of his nicknames was "The Rainbow Hunter." To Shane, every rainbow was a sign of something beautiful, something that reminded him—and everyone around him—that joy was just a glance away.

These tiny discoveries weren't just about seeing something special in the ordinary; they were symbols of his gentle, compassionate spirit. Each heart he found, each rainbow he pointed out, was his way of reminding others of the wonder in the world, even during life's most difficult moments.

With his signature blend of humor and sincerity, Shane had a way of making people feel lighter, even on the toughest of days. He'd crack a joke to lift a heavy heart, offer a sincere compliment when someone needed it most, or just quietly sit and listen with a knowing smile that seemed to say, "I'm here." Shane's gift was more than just a knack for spotting rainbows and hearts; it was his ability to remind people of the good around them. And just as he saw love and beauty in the world, he helped others see it too, one heart, one rainbow, and one laugh at a time.

This is a great lesson for all of us. Because there really is beauty in everything, and everyone has some positive quality that makes them unique. Shane just had a way of uncovering whatever that was and making sure that person knew it, so that he left them feeling better about themselves.

Perhaps if more people did this, the world would be a kinder place.

In sharing Shane's story, it's my hope that you, too, will feel inspired to look for those small, meaningful ways to bring love, laughter, and light into others' lives. Shane showed us that extraordinary impact lies not in grand gestures but in the quiet, often unnoticed acts of kindness that have the power to heal, uplift, and connect us all. This book is a testament to that legacy, a reminder that each of us can be an Earth Angel and have an extraordinary impact, creating beauty and kindness in the world in our own unique ways.

Finding Your Uniqueness— Your Superpowers

> *The saddest thing in life is wasted talent.*
> *—Chazz Palminteri*

Shane meeting actor Chazz Palminteri.

Each of us carries unique qualities, perspectives, and talents that, when fully embraced, become our superpowers. By recognizing and valuing what makes us different, we unlock strengths that can be used to make a meaningful impact in the world. This journey to uncovering our superpowers often starts with self-discovery—understanding what drives us and acknowledging the traits that make us who we are.

When we lean into these unique qualities, we not only grow personally but also find ways to help others, uplift communities, and inspire positive social change. In using our uniqueness as a guide, we can discover that our superpowers are often the very things that connect us with others and empower us to make a significant difference.

Eliminating Self-Doubt and Erasing Limiting Beliefs

Identifying your superpowers isn't possible without first clearing the path of self-doubt and limiting beliefs. These mental barriers cloud our perception, causing us to second-guess our abilities and shrink from our true potential. Self-doubt whispers that we're not enough, while limiting thoughts keep us boxed within the familiar, afraid to explore beyond. To uncover our superpowers, we have to shed these constraints, allowing clarity and confidence to emerge. Only by eliminating the weight of doubt can we fully recognize and harness the extraordinary capabilities we each carry within ourselves.

SELF-DOUBT

Self-doubt often appears as a critical inner voice, questioning our worth or abilities in comparison to others. In short, reining in feelings of self-doubt is essential to becoming your authentic self and unlocking your true superpowers. Self-doubt keeps us in a state of hesitation and creates a barrier between who we are and who we aspire to be, holding us back from fully expressing our unique talents and passions. By letting go of these doubts, we can explore our full potential without fear of judgment or failure. This openness allows our authentic self to shine, enabling us to use our strengths in ways that genuinely reflect who we really are.

Here are a few examples of self-doubt and how it affects our ability to live authentically:

Fear of judgment: Many people experience self-doubt when they worry about others' opinions, which can lead to hiding their true feelings, ideas, or ambitions. This fear pushes us to conform to others' expectations, ultimately stifling our genuine self-expression and leaving us disconnected from what we truly value.

Impostor syndrome: A common form of self-doubt is feeling like a "fraud" in our own achievements or capabilities. This can prevent us from pursuing new opportunities or showcasing our skills. Instead of embracing our talents, we hold back, missing out on personal growth and authentic connections.

Perfectionism: Self-doubt can make us feel that we're never good enough, driving perfectionist tendencies. This need for flawlessness creates immense pressure, and instead of presenting our genuine work or personality, we may overedit or hesitate to share at all, losing touch with what truly makes our contributions valuable.

Comparison to others: Self-doubt often arises when we measure ourselves against others, making us feel inadequate or insecure. This comparison dilutes our unique qualities as we try to mimic others' strengths rather than embracing our own, ultimately compromising our authentic identity.

Fear of rejection: Many people doubt their worthiness for relationships, opportunities, or even happiness, which can make them hesitant to pursue meaningful goals. This fear can cause them to settle for less, distancing them from their passions and potential.

By recognizing and overcoming these doubts, we create space for our authentic selves to flourish. Only then can we bring our unique perspectives and talents forward, enriching our own lives and those around us. When self-doubt fades, our superpowers begin to naturally emerge, guiding us toward a life aligned with our deepest values and aspirations.

LIMITING BELIEFS

Limiting beliefs are often deeply ingrained assumptions that act like invisible chains, holding us back from realizing our true potential and preventing us from embracing our authentic selves. These beliefs often stem from past experiences, social conditioning, or fears of inadequacy, and they block us from seeing our unique strengths.

By shedding these beliefs, we can create space for our authentic self to emerge unrestricted by doubt or preconceived boundaries. When we operate from a place of authenticity, our superpowers can become tools for connection, inspiration, and support, allowing us to contribute meaningfully to those around us.

When we begin to challenge and replace negative thoughts with empowering ones, this can eventually create a mindset that sees challenges as opportunities, not obstacles. Replacing limiting beliefs with empowering ones is a journey, but it's worth it for the freedom it brings, because it helps build resilience, confidence, and a sense of possibility, allowing us to see beyond perceived imitations.

By focusing on beliefs that lift you up instead of holding you back, you are one step closer to becoming the best version of yourself.

Examples of Limiting Beliefs Versus Empowering Beliefs

Limiting Belief	Empowering Belief
"I'm not good enough."	"I am constantly growing and improving."
"I don't deserve success."	"I deserve success and am capable of achieving it."
"I'll never be able to do this."	"With this time and effort, I can learn how to do this."
"I always fail when I try new things."	"Every attempt is a chance to learn and grow."
"I'm too old/young to start something new."	"It's never too late or early to pursue my goals."
"People will judge me if I make a mistake."	"Making mistakes is a part of learning, and I grow from them."
"I'm not creative."	"Creativity is a skill I can cultivate and develop."
"I'm not smart enough to succeed in this field."	"I am capable of learning and mastering new skills."
"I don't have enough time to pursue my passion."	"I can make time for what matters most to me."
"I'm afraid of failing."	"Failure is a stepping stone to success."

When you allow yourself to be fully and unapologetically who you are, you uncover unique strengths, passions, and talents that might otherwise remain hidden beneath layers of doubt or conformity. Authenticity clears away the distractions of comparison and societal expectations, allowing your natural abilities to shine. By embracing your true self, you can tap into a deeper sense of purpose and confidence, empowering you to leverage your superpowers in ways that are meaningful and impactful. In embracing authenticity, you unlock the full potential of what you're capable of and how you can contribute to the world.

> *You're always with yourself, so you might as well enjoy the company.*
> *—Diane von Furstenberg*

Discovering Your Superpowers

Your unique gifts, when shared, have the potential to inspire, uplift, and empower those around you, making you a hero in your own right. Discovering your personal superpowers is about embracing your authentic self and the unique ways you can contribute to the world. It's recognizing that you have the ability to make a difference, even in small, everyday actions. Without sounding trite, your superpowers aren't represented in a Marvel movie; rather, they're traits that make you a source of light, love, and healing in your own unique way—simply by being you.

> *The things you are passionate about are not random. They are your calling.*
> *—Fabienne Fredrickson*

CHAPTER SEVEN

While Earth Angels are everyday people, the following stories are examples of well-known people who use/have used their superpowers to make a positive impact by embracing their authentic uniqueness.

TEMPLE GRANDIN—VISUAL THINKING AND EMPATHY FOR ANIMALS

- **Superpower**: Temple Grandin, an animal scientist with autism, has an extraordinary ability to think visually, which allows her to understand animals' experiences in ways that others might overlook.

- **How she uses it**: Grandin revolutionized the livestock industry by designing humane animal handling systems, improving the lives of millions of animals. Her work has also increased awareness and understanding of autism, showing the world the unique insights those with autism can bring.

OPRAH WINFREY—EMPATHY AND STORYTELLING

- **Superpower**: Oprah's deep empathy and skill in storytelling allow her to connect with people on a personal level, making her one of the most influential media moguls in the world.

- **How she uses it**: By using her platform to share diverse stories, she's raised awareness on countless social issues and empowers and encourages millions to pursue self-improvement, ultimately creating a space for authentic, compassionate dialogue.

MALALA YOUSAFZAI—ADVOCACY FOR GIRLS' EDUCATION

- **Superpower**: Malala, despite facing threats and an attack by extremists, has used her courage to advocate for girls' right to education. She has become a global voice for the millions of girls around the world who are denied education.

- **How she uses it**: Through her foundation, the Malala Fund, she supports education projects and advocates for policy changes, helping empower young girls to access education and reach their potential.

MISTER ROGERS (FRED ROGERS)— COMPASSION AND EMPATHY

- **Superpower**: Fred Rogers used his deep sense of empathy to connect with children through his television show, *Mister Rogers' Neighborhood*. He addressed difficult topics such as loss, anger, and fear in a way that was accessible and comforting to children.

- **How he used it**: By creating a space where children felt understood and valued, Rogers taught multiple generations about kindness, acceptance, and emotional intelligence, shaping countless young lives with his gentle wisdom.

DOLLY PARTON—PHILANTHROPY AND LITERACY PROGRAMS

- **Superpower**: Dolly Parton uses her platform and resources to promote literacy and a love of reading through the Imagination Library, which provides free books to children worldwide. Dolly also gives back through numerous charitable efforts, especially those focused on education and community support.

- **How she uses it:** Parton has also contributed to healthcare, funding research at Vanderbilt University for a COVID-19 vaccine, and she actively supports her local community in East Tennessee through various donations, scholarships, and disaster relief efforts. Dolly's philanthropy is deeply rooted in a desire to uplift others and invest in future generations.

BRANDON STANTON—STORYTELLING THROUGH *HUMANS OF NEW YORK*

- **Superpower**: Stanton, the creator of *Humans of New York*, has used his talent for storytelling to share the stories of everyday people from around the world, offering a platform for voices that might otherwise go unheard.

- **How he uses it**: By sharing these stories, Brandon has raised awareness of various social issues and has connected people from diverse backgrounds. He has also used his platform to raise funds for causes and individuals in need, turning stories into real-world support.

BRYAN STEVENSON—FIGHTING FOR JUSTICE

- **Superpower**: Stevenson, the founder of the Equal Justice Initiative, has dedicated his life to challenging racial and economic injustice in the legal system, focusing on those who have been wrongly convicted or unfairly sentenced.

- **How he uses it**: Stevenson provides legal representation to those in need, educates the public about systemic inequalities, and has contributed to the creation of the National Memorial for Peace and Justice. His work has led to significant reforms in criminal justice.

JOSÉ ANDRÉS—FEEDING COMMUNITIES IN CRISIS

- **Superpower**: Chef José Andrés founded the nonprofit World Central Kitchen, which provides meals in the wake of natural disasters and humanitarian crises.

- **How he uses it**: Using his culinary skills and ability to quickly organize, he has provided millions of meals to people affected by hurricanes, earthquakes, and other emergencies, ensuring that communities in crisis receive nourishment and care.

JANE GOODALL—CONSERVATION AND ANIMAL RIGHTS

- **Superpower**: Goodall's work with chimpanzees has transformed how we understand animals and conservation. Her dedication has turned her into a global advocate for wildlife preservation and environmental awareness.

- **How she uses it**: Through the Jane Goodall Institute, Goodall promotes conservation, sustainable living, and youth programs that empower young people to become leaders in environmental stewardship.

CHADWICK BOSEMAN—INSPIRING THROUGH REPRESENTATION

- **Superpower**: As an actor, Boseman chose roles that highlighted Black heroes and figures of historical importance, from Jackie Robinson to T'Challa in *Black Panther.*

- **How he used it**: Through his performances, Boseman inspired millions by providing powerful representation on screen, showing young people, especially those from marginalized communities, that they too can be heroes. Even while battling cancer, he used his platform to uplift and bring hope to others.

As beautiful as these stories may be, Earth Angels don't have to be famous to create positive change; more often than not, they are ordinary people quietly making a difference in the lives of those around them. These individuals embody kindness, compassion, and resilience, without the expectation of recognition. Their strength lies in their authenticity and selflessness, reminding us that anyone, regardless of fame or status, has the power to bring hope, support, and love to others.

Here are some inspiring examples of everyday people who discovered their superpowers in seemingly ordinary qualities and used them to make a meaningful difference—Earth Angels.

THE TEACHER WHO EMPOWERED STUDENTS TO BELIEVE IN THEMSELVES

- **Superpower**: A high school teacher with an innate ability to listen, encourage, and connect with students.

- **How they used it**: This teacher noticed that many students lacked confidence and direction. By dedicating time to listening to their struggles and offering words of encouragement, they inspired students to pursue their passions. Their belief in their students' potential became a catalyst for the students' success and growth, shaping their lives with compassion and empathy.

THE NEIGHBOR WITH A KNACK FOR ORGANIZING AND A LOVE FOR COMMUNITY

- **Superpower**: A community-oriented individual with exceptional organizational skills.
- **How they used it**: Seeing isolation during the pandemic, this neighbor organized a neighborhood support network, arranging meal deliveries for those who couldn't leave their homes and coordinating online meetups. Their ability to organize people and resources brought neighbors closer, fostered friendships, and provided essential support to the vulnerable.

THE MECHANIC WITH A HEART FOR HELPING SINGLE PARENTS

- **Superpower**: A mechanic with a talent for fixing cars and a compassionate heart.
- **How they used it**: Realizing how many single parents in their community struggled with car repairs, this mechanic began offering free services on weekends. What started as small acts of kindness grew into a network of support, allowing families to save money and stay safe on the road.

THE RETIREE WHO BROUGHT JOY TO SKILLED NURSING FACILITY RESIDENTS

- **Superpower**: A retiree with the gift of storytelling and patience.

- **How they used it**: This retiree began volunteering at a local skilled nursing facility, spending time with residents who had limited family connections. Through storytelling, sharing experiences, and listening, they brought joy, comfort, and companionship to residents, transforming their days and brightening spirits with the power of empathy.

THE TEENAGER WHO TURNED A PASSION FOR BAKING INTO FUNDRAISING

- **Superpower**: A teenager with a passion for baking and a commitment to giving back.

- **How they used it**: Inspired to support a local animal shelter, this young baker started selling homemade treats, donating all proceeds to help animals in need. What began as a hobby turned into a way to make an impact, combining a love of baking with a desire to help others.

Each of these individuals discovered a unique aspect of themselves—a passion, a perspective, or talent to create positive change, showing that their uniqueness, their superpowers, don't have to be complicated to make an extraordinary impact, they just need to be authentic.

Here are some tips to help you discover and harness the powers that only you possess.

Identify your natural gifts: Reflect on the things that come naturally to you, especially those that bring you joy or give you a sense of purpose. It could be your ability to listen deeply, your compassion for others, or your knack for solving problems.

Pay attention to what moves you: Notice what makes you feel excited, passionate, or alive. It could be helping others, solving problems, creating art, or listening to someone in need. These moments are clues to your strengths.

Reflect on your challenges: Sometimes, our struggles and challenges reveal our strengths. Consider the hardships you've faced and how you overcame them. The resilience, wisdom, and empathy you've developed through those experiences can be a powerful part of your mission.

Practice self-reflection: Take time to think about times when you've felt most fulfilled or proud of yourself. What were you doing? What strengths were you using? Reflection can help you connect the dots between what you love and where your gifts lie.

Experiment and explore: Don't be afraid to try new things or step into unfamiliar roles. Sometimes we discover our superpowers in the least expected places when we give ourselves permission to step outside of our comfort zones.

Self-love and self-acceptance: As I wrote about earlier in this chapter, part of discovering your superpowers is recognizing that you are enough just as you are. When you accept yourself fully, including your quirks and imperfections, you become more aligned with your true purpose.

CHAPTER SEVEN

Using Your Superpowers

> *When I stand before God at the end of my life, I would hope that I would not have a single bit of talent left and could say, I used everything you gave me.*
> —Erma Bombeck

Using your superpowers holds the key to creating positive change. When you live out your superpowers authentically and consistently, you can inspire others to do the same. By showing resilience, integrity, or creativity in your actions, you encourage those around you to cultivate these qualities within themselves—the ripple effect again.

I know someone who got a terrible call at work. She was being bullied by her ex-husband, and he was yelling and threatening her about their five-year-old daughter. Because the workplace was a cubicle setup, despite her efforts to be quiet, her crying could be heard by her colleague nearby. This cubicle neighbor, whose superpowers were gentleness and thoughtfulness, quietly and discreetly went and made a cup of hot tea for her crying coworker (whom she did not know well) and set it on her desk along with a box of Kleenex. She then returned to her own cubicle. Later, she left a Post-it for her neighbor saying, "If you need someone to just listen, I am right next door."

The thing that resonates is that this story is not at all about a grand gesture. It was a simple, quiet act of kindness by an Earth Angel. By the way, this happened twenty-five years ago, and my friend *still* tells this story as an example of "someone who walks the walk." To this day, she is still impacted by this small gesture of sincere kindness.

> *Kind words can be short and easy to speak, but their echoes are truly endless.*
> —Mother Teresa

Creating social change by embracing and using our superpowers requires a collective effort. By actively incorporating these actions into our daily lives and encouraging others to do the same, we can each contribute to creating a more compassionate and kinder world.

Earth Angels Can Heal Our World

Earth Angels are not defined by fame or grandeur, but by their willingness to act with intention and purpose. Even the smallest, seemingly insignificant gesture can serve as the catalyst for positive change. A kind word, a thoughtful action, or a moment of compassion can influence someone for years, becoming a part of their life story and potentially shaping how they treat others.

Most of us have heard of the term "the butterfly effect," which sounds simple, but it is actually a concept from chaos theory. In very basic terms, one small action (the flapping of a butterfly's wings) can have enormous consequences. I've used the metaphor of a ripple across a pond. Identifying your superpowers as an Earth Angel—the flapping of your wings—can impact others in ways you may never become aware of. Someone once described it to me like an elaborate domino setup. When the first tile plinks over and starts that chain reaction, the small motion of that single domino causes an enormous effect. Your small act of kindness, or a thoughtful word, might change someone else's life . . . who, in turn, might then change someone else's, and so on. What goes around comes around.

What differentiates an Earth Angel is intent. They don't do things for recognition but out of genuineness and a desire to make the world a better place. Like Shane collecting hearts and rainbows as he looked around the world, or when he gave away his Play-Doh set to the toddler who didn't yet understand winning from losing. If you actively *look* for the Earth Angels around you, you will see acts that restore faith in humanity. These are what can heal our world.

Here are more inspiring stories that show how simple acts of everyday kindness have made a positive impact.

THE POWER OF A SIMPLE THANK YOU NOTE

A man named Chris noticed that a bus driver always greeted everyone with a smile and kind words, despite the stressful nature of the job. Chris decided to write a heartfelt thank you note to the driver, expressing appreciation for his positivity. The bus driver was deeply moved and shared that he had been struggling with personal challenges and felt invisible. The note reminded him that his small acts of kindness were noticed and valued, uplifting his spirit and motivating him to keep spreading positivity.

PAYING FOR GROCERIES LEADS TO A CHAIN REACTION

During the COVID-19 pandemic, a woman named Susan noticed an elderly man struggling to pay for his groceries. Without hesitation, she paid for his items. The man was overwhelmed with gratitude and shared that he was unsure how he would get by that week. Susan's act of kindness inspired several other customers in line to start paying for others' groceries. This small gesture turned into a community effort, with neighbors helping neighbors and offering support during difficult times.

THE IMPACT OF A WARM WINTER COAT

A teacher in a low-income school district noticed that one of her students, a young girl, was coming to school without a proper winter coat. The teacher discreetly bought her a warm coat, gloves, and hat. The girl's demeanor changed immediately—she was happier, more engaged in class, and even started making friends. The warmth and comfort of the coat didn't just help her physically; it gave her confidence and a sense of belonging.

A STRANGER'S KINDNESS SAVES A LIFE

A man named John was feeling hopeless and had decided to take his own life. On the way to his intended destination, a stranger struck up a conversation with him, offering him coffee and kind words. The stranger didn't know John was struggling, but his genuine interest made John rethink his decision. John later shared his story online, crediting that brief moment of connection with saving his life. The stranger's kindness reminded him that there were still people who cared, even if they were strangers.

A COMMUNITY RALLIES AROUND A TEACHER

A beloved teacher named Mrs. Thompson was diagnosed with a serious illness and had to undergo expensive treatments. Her former students, many of whom had been positively influenced by her kindness and dedication over the years, organized a fundraiser. They spread the word through social media, and the campaign quickly grew, raising more than enough money for her medical bills. Mrs. Thompson was overwhelmed by the support, and the community's kindness gave her strength during a difficult time.

CHAPTER SEVEN

A CUP OF COFFEE LEADS TO A JOB OPPORTUNITY

A young man was sitting in a café, struggling to update his résumé. He was feeling discouraged after months of unemployment. A woman nearby noticed his frustration and offered to buy him a coffee. They struck up a conversation, and it turned out she worked in human resources. She offered to review his résumé and suggested a few job opportunities at her company. A week later, he received a job offer. The simple act of offering coffee turned into a life-changing opportunity for the young man.

A CHILD'S GENEROSITY CHANGES AN UNHOUSED MAN'S LIFE

A nine-year-old girl named Ella noticed an unhoused man near her school and felt compelled to help. She decided to save her allowance and brought him a warm meal, along with a handwritten note that said, "You are loved." The man was moved to tears and shared that it had been a long time since he felt seen or valued. Touched by her kindness, he started seeking help at a local shelter and eventually found housing and a job. Ella's small gesture of love gave him the hope and motivation he needed to rebuild his life.

KINDNESS TRANSFORMS A NEIGHBORHOOD

In a neighborhood where people barely interacted, a woman named Sarah started leaving small notes of encouragement on her neighbors' doors, along with baked goods. Her kind gestures started conversations and brought people together. Soon, other neighbors joined in, and they organized block parties, community cleanups, and support groups. What was once a disconnected community became a close-knit group where people looked out for each other, all sparked by one person's simple acts of kindness.

As we conclude this chapter on finding your superpowers, I can't help but think of Shane and the quiet strength he carried. Shane's superpowers included his ability to bring light into every room, to find beauty in the smallest of things, and to make others feel seen and valued. He had a rare gift for lifting spirits, reminding people that they mattered, even when he was struggling himself. Losing Shane has left a void, a profound reminder of how precious and impactful a single life can be. But his legacy—his laughter, his smile, his kindness, his way of seeing hearts and rainbows—remains.

His life teaches us that compassion and kindness can change lives, sometimes most powerfully when they're offered by those who understand suffering themselves. Shane's story is a testament to the strength it takes to keep spreading love, even when the world feels heavy, and to the extraordinary courage it takes to be a light for others, even while carrying hidden pain. For our superpowers don't need to be flashy or grand; often, they're found in the way we treat others, in how we show up, and in the ways that we choose to share our gifts. Shane's life reminds us that these powers, however simple they may seem, have the potential to change lives and create ripples that go on long after we're gone.

In honoring Shane's memory, I hope that you, too, will look within to find your own superpowers and use them to make a positive impact. Let his story be a guide—a reminder that even the smallest acts of love and kindness are powerful, and that we all have the capacity to be someone's Earth Angel.

You only have one shot, so please make it *mean* something.

Every day is a journey.

Every day, you are faced with choices.

Every day is an opportunity to be an Earth Angel.

conclusion

embracing the earth angel within and inspiring kindness

The only person you are destined to become is the person you decide to be.
—RALPH WALDO EMERSON

In this final chapter, we come full circle to the power of small, everyday actions. Throughout this journey, we've seen how kindness, resilience, and compassion—the simplest of qualities—have the potential to transform lives and create ripples of positive change. Here, we reflect on the enduring impact of these small acts, understanding that real power lies in the ordinary moments we often take for granted. Each of us holds the ability to uplift, inspire, and bring light to others, proving that extraordinary impact is within reach for anyone reading this book and willing to lead with an open heart.

Shane is no longer here as an Earth Angel, but his spirit and the impact of his kindness live on. My deepest hope is that Shane's story has touched your heart and inspired you to see the incredible power within your own everyday actions. Shane has shown us that it doesn't take grand gestures to make a difference: sometimes, the simplest acts of kindness and compassion can have the most lasting impact. His life serves as a reminder that each of us, in our own way, can be an Earth Angel to someone else. Let his legacy encourage you to act with intention, to bring light to those around you, and to recognize the profound impact that even the simplest of actions can have. May you go forward, empowered to make a difference, knowing that by becoming an Earth Angel, you're creating a world filled with more love, kindness, and hope.

Through his quiet acts of compassion, Shane embodied what it means to be an Earth Angel. His life was a reminder that you don't need fame, fortune, or a title to make a difference, just an open heart and the willingness to see others' needs. He taught us that simple moments of kindness can be transformative, inspiring those around us to find and share their own inner light.

May we all carry his legacy forward, recognizing the importance of kindness and the profound impact we can have on one another.

But the journey doesn't end here. This book is an invitation—for each of us to recognize our own potential to be an Earth Angel. It's a call to let go of self-doubt, embrace our superpowers, and step forward authentically, knowing that our efforts can make a difference. The power to inspire kindness and create change lies within us all, and every act of compassion, no matter how small, adds to a wave of positivity that can ripple across communities and far beyond.

Together: The Earth Angel Pledge

Let's actively *do* something to combat this problem. Let's come together and make a difference. I created a pledge, where each piece is part of an acronym for EARTH ANGEL. When I first wrote the pledge, my initial plan was to create it as a series, each tailored for different groups: organizations/workplaces, adults, kids, and parents—each relevant to their unique environments. However, as I wrote this book and reflected on its core message, it became clear that the Earth Angel principles transcend these categories. Each part of the pledge's content resonates universally, offering a guide for kindness, empathy, and positive impact that anyone can embrace. This realization shifted my vision, hopefully making the pledge something that connects us all, regardless of age, role, or background.

THE EARTH ANGEL PLEDGE

This pledge emphasizes the power of daily actions, encouraging a lifestyle that is mindful, generous, and focused on the well-being of all. It serves as a reminder that each of us has the ability to make the world a better place, one small act at a time, as an EARTH ANGEL.

EMPOWER

I will empower those around me, encouraging others to see their potential and believe in themselves.

ACCEPT

I pledge to accept myself, just as I am. I am perfectly imperfect, and I will remember that what makes me different is what makes the world a better place.

Respect

I will treat everyone with respect, kindness, and dignity, even though their values and opinions may be different from my own.

Think

I pledge to think before I speak, act, or post online, considering how my words and actions can impact others.

Human

I pledge to remember that we are all human, each of us facing private battles that deserve compassion and understanding.

Authentic

I pledge to be authentic, staying true to myself and my values in all that I do.

Nonjudgmental

I pledge to be nonjudgmental, recognizing that people are so much more than what we see on the surface.

Gratitude

I pledge to live with gratitude, focusing on the blessings I have rather than what I lack.

Encourage

I pledge to encourage others, offering support and positivity to help them thrive.

Lead by example

I pledge to lead by example, demonstrating integrity and kindness in all my actions.

It is my hope that the Earth Angel pledge will serve as a daily reminder to embody these principles with purpose, guiding each of us to live with empathy, authenticity, and kindness. By committing to this pledge, we each commit to becoming a positive force in the world, inspiring others and ourselves to lead lives of compassion and integrity.

In a world that often feels uncertain, the kindness of Earth Angels shines like a beacon, reminding us of our shared humanity and the simple yet profound impact of caring for one another. So, as you close this book, please remember this: you have the ability to light the way for others. By embracing the Earth Angel within you, you become a part of a growing circle of compassion, one that has the power to heal, uplift, and inspire kindness in countless others.

Shane is forever perfect. Forever eleven years old. Forever a bright star, a heart, a rainbow.

To this day, I continue to receive messages from people around the world whose lives were touched by Shane's innocence and kindness. His genuine spirit and warmth left a lasting impact, creating memories that people still carry with them. Each message is a reminder of the quiet, yet profound influence he had on others, simply by being himself. His kindness resonates beyond borders, connecting us all in a shared appreciation for the beauty of a compassionate heart.

As we reach the end of *Earth Angels*, I want to thank you, dear reader, for taking this journey with me. Your willingness to walk through these stories, to reflect on the moments of kindness and resilience, means more than words can express. I hope that Shane's lessons—the beauty of innocence, the power of kindness, and the impact of a compassionate heart—will remain with you always. Let us honor his legacy by embracing these lessons every day, remembering that each of us has the power to be an Earth Angel in someone else's life.

Thank you for allowing his spirit to touch yours.

Kind is the new cool.

remembering shane resnick

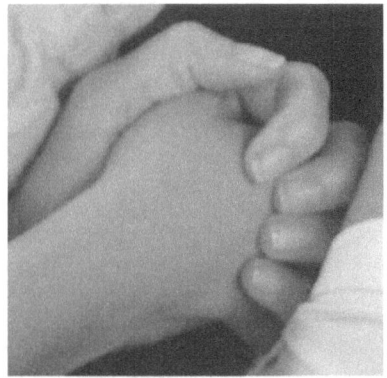

A tender moment captured in time. Shane with his small hand wrapped tightly around mine as we waited for one of his brothers. The bond we shared was as natural as breathing, always holding hands without a second thought. I teased him, saying, "One day you'll be too embarrassed to hold my hand." He looked at me with unwavering sincerity and said, "I will never be too embarrassed to hold your hand." It was a promise spoken with the purest heart, a reflection of the love that defined him.

EARTH ANGELS

A poignant snapshot of Shane's last first day of school—a moment filled with pride, joy, and hope. His smile radiates pure happiness, his eyes sparkling with excitement for the year ahead. The warmth and light he exuded seemed almost larger than life, making it unimaginable that such a vibrant presence would be taken away months later. This photo holds both the beauty of his spirit and the heartbreak of his absence, a reminder of the irreplaceable light that was stolen from us far too soon.

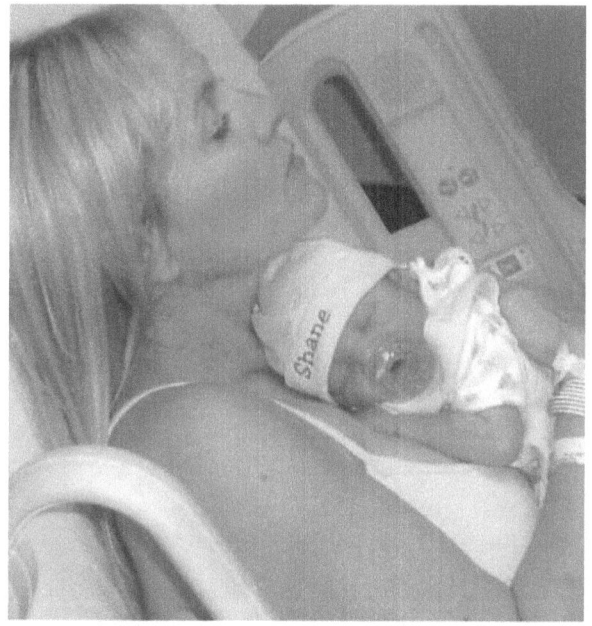

A photo that captures the beginning of a bond like no other: me holding Shane minutes after he entered the world. His tiny body nestled against mine, his presence already filling the room with love and wonder. Over the years, he would often say to me, "Mom. I could have been born to anyone or anywhere in the world. I'm so glad I was born to you." In this moment, looking at his perfect little face, I already knew I felt the same exact way.

A photo of all three boys, standing together and dressed in identical outfits—a picture of innocence, brotherhood, and love. I always dressed them alike anytime we were out in public, a choice rooted in my deep protective instinct. My worst fear—ironically—was something happening to one of them. Dressing them the same gave me a sense of control, a way to ensure that if one ever went missing, I could hold another up and say, "This is what to look for." This picture, while sweet and endearing, now carries a bittersweet weight, a reminder of both my love for them and the unimaginable loss that came to pass.

A close-up photo of Shane's eyes from the year he passed—so striking and unique, they seemed to tell stories all on their own. I always told him he had the most beautiful eyes, a shape unlike anyone else's on either side of our families. They held a depth, a light that made them unforgettable, as if they were windows into his extraordinary soul. Looking at this photo now, it's impossible not to be captivated by their beauty and wonder how much they saw, felt, and held in silence. His eyes were truly one of a kind, just like him.

Shane had an unshakeable love for amusement parks from the moment he could walk, with a particular fascination for rollercoasters. His passion went beyond riding them—he memorized every rollercoaster in the world, proudly reciting their heights, speeds, and unique features. Before going to an amusement park, he would memorize its layout (from an online map) so we could maximize our time strategically. Fear was never in his vocabulary when it came to rollercoasters; he was ready for every twist and drop. At every pediatrician visit, his first request was always to have his height measured—not for medical reasons but to excitedly calculate which rollercoasters he'd be tall enough to conquer next. His boundless enthusiasm is shown in this photo of Shane pretending to be on a rollercoaster in my laundry basket. The picture captures who he was: inventive, curious, and endlessly driven by the things he loved.

REMEMBERING SHANE RESNICK

A sweet photo of Shane grinning widely with a gap where his bottom tooth had been. That night, he went to bed buzzing with excitement and the anticipation of waking up with a gift from the Tooth Fairy under his pillow. But I had asked him to pick up the toys on his bedroom floor—a request he didn't fulfill. So I left a playful letter from the Tooth Fairy under his pillow, explaining that she couldn't leave her gift because of the clutter. The next morning, I braced myself for disappointment, but instead, Shane bounced down the stairs, letter in hand. He handed me the letter and cheerfully declared, "It's OK. I'll just clean up my room today, and she'll come tonight!" This photo captures not just his excitement, but also his beautiful outlook on life. Shane had a rare ability to turn setbacks into opportunities, always looking at the bright side, and his boundless positivity and sense of humor made moments like these unforgettable.

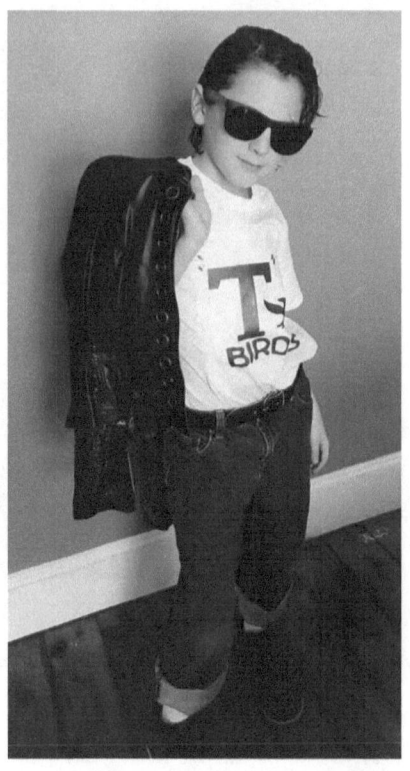

A photo of Shane just before his last school event, dressed in a perfectly curated 1950s-inspired outfit for his fifth-grade theme. His (what I thought to be) confidence radiates outward, a picture of pride and readiness for the event. Looking at it now, it's unfathomable to think he was suffering in silence. The effort and love poured into every detail of his costume reflect how much I always wanted my boys to feel proud and supported. Yet, behind that assumed confidence, there was a pain I couldn't see—a heartbreaking reminder of how deeply he tried to protect those around him, even as he struggled within.

acknowledgments

To all the Earth Angels around the world—this book is dedicated to you. Your quiet acts of kindness, your compassion, and your selfless contributions remind us that the greatest impact often comes from those who seek nothing in return.

To all the people silently suffering, I want to remind you that you matter. You are perfectly imperfect—just the way you are.

Thank you to the many people who have inspired the stories in this book. Whether you are a teacher who stayed after school to help a struggling student, a nurse who provided comfort beyond the call of duty, or a neighbor who lent a helping hand without being asked—you are the reason this book exists.

A special thanks to my family and friends who have walked beside me, inspiring me with their generosity of spirit. And to those whose names may never be known but whose hearts make the world a better place, your example teaches us that kindness is the most powerful force we have.

about the author

Sandy Lundy is a community leader whose work has been deeply influenced by personal tragedy. In 2018, Sandy's eleven-year-old son Shane took his own life after having been bullied. Sandy has spoken about the unfathomable pain her family experienced and how she has made a conscious decision to channel that pain into something meaningful.

Sandy's dedication to her sons is a central theme in her advocacy work and is a powerful aspect of this book. Sandy's story and work have garnered local and national attention as part of a broader effort to honor her son and protect other children from similar pain.

Her initiatives reflect her admiration for those who contribute to positive change quietly but meaningfully. Sandy has dedicated her efforts to building a network of compassionate individuals who inspire others through small acts of kindness, reinforcing that these everyday heroes (Earth Angels) are integral to creating a world where kindness becomes the norm. These Earth Angels align with her belief that changing the world starts with simple, heartfelt gestures that inevitably create a ripple effect.

in loving memory of ...

Shane Resnick
Bob Brunner
Jimmy Plitnick
Raymond "Jeeter" Lundy
Roy Teverbaugh

www.ingramcontent.com/pod-product-compliance
Lightning Source LLC
Chambersburg PA
CBHW030219170426
43194CB00007BA/796